THE CATHOLIC UNIV

Some Aspects of the Horse and Rider Analogy in *The Debate between the Body and the Soul*

A DISSERTATION

SUBMITTED TO THE FACULTY OF THE GRADUATE SCHOOL OF ARTS AND SCIENCES OF THE CATHOLIC UNIVERSITY OF AMERICA IN PARTIAL FULFILLMENT OF THE REQUIREMENTS FOR THE DEGREE OF DOCTOR OF PHILOSOPHY

BY

SISTER MARY URSULA VOGEL

OF

THE SCHOOL SISTERS OF ST. FRANCIS
MILWAUKEE, WISCONSIN

THE CATHOLIC UNIVERSITY OF AMERICA PRESS, INC.
WASHINGTON, D. C.
1948

Copyright, 1948
THE CATHOLIC UNIVERSITY OF AMERICA PRESS, INC.

PRINTED IN THE UNITED STATES OF AMERICA
BY THE SERAPHIC PRESS, MILWAUKEE, WIS.

PREFACE

The present study of some aspects of the analogy of the horse and the horseman in *The Debate between the Body and the Soul* is the result of one phase of a more general investigation of the Body and Soul theme, which had its origin in a seminar devoted to an intensive inquiry into the morality plays. The contextual study of one of these plays, *Mankind*,[1] reveals the significant rôle of the debate of the Body and Soul motif in its structure, and there is definite evidence that two other plays, the *Castle of Perseverance*[2] and the *Pride of Life*,[3] disclose its use in their structure.

By means of the metaphor of the horse and rider the poet of *The Debate between the Body and the Soul* concretizes the abstract meaning of soul, the seat of the intellect and will, as that faculty of man which bears the responsibility of sin. He conceives the soul as having taken up its abode somehow and somewhere inside the bodily frame and from there ruling and guiding it. The soul as rider holds the reins. But the history of the image reveals by implication that the words *horse* and *rider* take on a serious burden of meaning when considered psychologically in terms of the essence of man.

The present study attempts to outline the general structure of *The Debate between the Body and the Soul* to determine the function of the horse-and-rider metaphor in the structure, to trace its history, and finally to analyze and evaluate it by setting it against the background of the teaching of Saint Thomas Aquinas.

---

[1] Sister Mary Philippa Coogan, *An Interpretation of the Moral Play, "Mankind,"* Ph.D. Dissertation of The Catholic University of America (Washington: The Catholic University of America Press, 1947), pp. 29, 75, 88.

[2] Tempe E. Allison, "On the Body and Soul Legend in the *Castle of Perseverance*," *MLN*, XLII (1927), 102 ff.

[3] Robert Lee Ramsay, Skelton's *Magnyfycence*, (London: EETS ES, 98, 1906), p. clxiii.

I wish to express my gratitude to Sister M. Emmanuel Collins, O.S.F., for suggesting the study of the Body and Soul theme in medieval literature and for giving me aid and encouragement as the work progressed; to Dr. James Craig LaDrière and the late Dr. Francis J. Hemelt for critical reading of the manuscript; and to Dr. Eleanor Kellogg Henningham for directing my attention to the work she has pursued in Body and Soul literature. I appreciate the courtesies extended to me by the librarians of the Mullen Library, Catholic University; of the Library of Congress; of the University of Chicago; and of the Newberry Library, Chicago. I am especially indebted to Reverend Mother M. Corona, O.S.F., and the Sisters of my Community for the opportunity of study at the Catholic University, an opportunity for which I am deeply grateful.

Feast of the Purification
February 2, 1948

TABLE OF CONTENTS

	PAGE
Preface	v
Table of Contents	vii
List of Abbreviations	ix

CHAPTER

I. The General Character of *The Debate between the Body and the Soul* 1

    Manuscript: History and Date 1

    Nature of the Debate 3

    General Structure of the Debate 7

    History of the Horse and Rider Image 31

II. The Psychological Meaning of the Analogy 38

III. The Ethical Meaning of the Analogy 58

IV. Conclusion 83

Appendix 87

Bibliography 103

Index 111

LIST OF ABBREVIATIONS

BGPM	*Beiträge zur Geschichte der Philosophie und Theologie des Mittelalters*
EETS OS	*Early English Text Society, Original Series*
EETS ES	*Early English Text Society, Extra Series*
JEGP	*Journal of English and Germanic Philology*
MLN	*Modern Language Notes*
MLR	*Modern Language Review*
NED	*New English Dictionary*
PG	*Patrologiæ Græca* (Migne)
PL	*Patrologiæ Latina* (Migne)
PMLA	*Publications of the Modern Language Association*

CHAPTER I

THE GENERAL CHARACTER OF
THE DEBATE BETWEEN THE BODY AND THE SOUL

MANUSCRIPT: HISTORY AND DATE

The Middle English debate, *The Debate between the Body and the Soul*, which scholars have on occasion termed the best embodiment of the theme in any literature[1] and the most poetical,[2] exists, as far as is known, in seven manuscripts,[3] all derived from one original manuscript. The "Auchinleck MS," fols. 31v ff., which dates from the beginning of the fourteenth century, contains seventy-four stanzas. The last five have been cut from the text and appear in miniature on the back of the sheets but only the beginning of each verse. The *Laud MS 108*, fols. 200v ff., Bodleian, which dates, perhaps, from the beginning of the fourteenth century, contains sixty-one stanzas, with four Old French verses next to an Old French sentence after stanza fifty-nine. The "Vernon MS," fols. 285v ff., Bodleian, of the

---

[1] G. L. Kittredge, in Introduction to the *Debate of the Body and the Soul*, modernized by F. J. Child (Boston: R. E. Lee Company, 1908), p. ix.

[2] W. H. Schofield, *English Literature from the Norman Conquest to Chaucer* (New York: The Macmillan Company, 1906), p. 426.

[3] Carleton Brown, *A Register of Middle English Religious and Didactic Verse* (Oxford: Clarendon Press, 1920), II, 48. See J. E. Wells, *A Manual of Writings in Middle English*, 1050-1400 (New Haven: Yale University Press, 1916), p. 412; Wilhelm Linow, *Þe Desputisoun bitwen þe Bodi and þe Soule*, Erlanger Beiträge zur Englischen Philologie I (1889), Part I, 3-4; Hermann Varnhagen, *Anglia: Zeitschrift für Englische Philologie* II (1879), 226-228. Wells, Linow, and Varnhagen mention only six manuscripts. Another Middle English poem, an entirely different piece in four-line stanzas, beginning "In an þestrei stude ic stod," has for its theme the debate of the Body and the Soul. It is preserved in Trinity College, Cambridge, *MS 323*, in *MS Digby 86*, and in *MS Harley 2253;* see Carleton Brown, *A Register of Middle English Religious and Didactic Verse*, II, 136. This poem, which stands quite apart from the debate we are discussing, is a reworking of the address type. See also Beatrice Allen, "The Debate of the Body and Soul in *MS Digby 86*, Miscellaneous Notes," *MLR*, XXII (1927), 189.

last fourth of the fourteenth century, has sixty-two stanzas; the *Digby MS 102*, fols. 136r ff., British Museum, from the beginning of the fifteenth century, sixty-seven stanzas; the *Royal MS 18 A X*, fols. 61v ff., British Museum, of the second half of the fourteenth or the beginning of the fifteenth century, sixty-seven stanzas; the "Simeon MS" (B. M. *Additional MS 22283*), fols. 800 ff., of the last fourth of the fourteenth century; and the B. M. *Additional MS 37787* fols. 34r ff. Only the first 198 verses of the "Simeon MS" are preserved and they coincide almost entirely with the *Royal* text. Whether, as is commonly thought, the "Simeon MS" is a copy of the "Vernon MS," or whether both are a copy of another now lost manuscript, must still remain an open question.[4]

Of these texts of the poem all but those of the fragmentary "Simeon MS" and the B. M. *Additional 37787* have appeared in print. The most accessible edition is that of Wilhelm Linow,[5] which includes texts from the "Auchinleck MS," the *Laud*, the "Vernon," and the *Digby*.[6] The "Auchinleck MS" first appeared in *Owain and Miles and other unedited Fragments of Ancient English Poetry*, edited by David and Laing and Others; the *Laud*, in the *Latin Poems Commonly attributed to Walter Mapes*, edited by Thomas Wright and printed for the Camden Society (London: 1841), pp. 334 ff.; in Eduard Mätzner's *Altenglische Sprachproben* I (Berlin: Weidmann'sche Buchhandlung, 1867), 92 ff., and another by Parker, which is a reprint of Linow's. Wright's edition was included in O. Emerson (ed.) *A Middle English Reader* (London: Macmillan, 1905), pp. 47 ff. The "Vernon MS" appeared in the *Latin Poems Commonly attributed to Walter Mapes*, pp. 340 ff.; the

---

[4] Linow, *loc. cit.;* Varnhagen, *loc. cit.*

[5] *Op. cit.*, pp. 24-195. Preceding the texts is an important introduction containing the discussion of the possible sources, the language, and the manuscript relationships of the *Desputisoun*, with emphasis on the French influence.

[6] The "Auchinleck" and *Laud* texts are placed parallel on pp. 24-65 and the "Vernon" and *Digby* on pp. 66-105.

Royal MS by Varnhagen in *Anglia: Zeitschrift für Englische Philologie,* II, 229 ff. Varnhagen appends to his edition Mätzner's remarks and collation of the *Laud* text. In 1892 Otto Kunze published a critical edition of *þe Desputisoun bitwen þe Bodi and þe Soule* as an inaugural dissertation at the university of Berlin.

Knowledge of the exact date of the composition is hardly forthcoming, as the contents of *The Debate between the Body and the Soul* offer no indication as to a definite time.[7] The oldest MSS, the "Auchinleck" and the *Laud,* which stem from the beginning of the fourteenth century, furnish a *terminus ad quem;* Linow would place the *terminus a quo* beyond the middle of the thirteenth century because of the great French influence. In the impossibility of fixing a definite date for the composition, Linow would place it in the second half of the thirteenth century.[8]

NATURE OF THE DEBATE

The Debate between the Body and the Soul belongs to the literary genre known as the debate,[9] a form so characteristic of the twelfth and early thirteenth centuries [10] that

---

[7] In the light of the *Laud MS,* Thomas Wright (*The Poems Commonly attributed to Walter Mapes,* p. 322) would assign the date somewhere in the thirteenth century. George Marsh [*Origin and History of the English Language* (New York: Charles Scribner, 1862), p. 240] is inclined to believe that the date is more recent on the basis of the dialect which he considers grammatically more modern than that of any other writer before Chaucer. Eduard Mätzner (p. 91) would place the debate in the first half of the thirteenth century because of its linguistic similarity to such works as "Ormulum," "Bestiary," "Genesis," "Exodus," and *Ancren Riwle.* J. Heesch [*Ueber Sprache und Versbau des halbsächsischen Gedichts, þe Desputisoun bitwen þe Bodi and þe Soule,* Kieler Dissertation (Kiel, 1884), p. 3] says it is a work of the transition period, 1150 to 1250.

[8] *Op. cit.,* p. 21. Linow is supported in his conclusions by Otto Kunze, p. 40. See *supra,* p. 3.

[9] Sister M. Emmanuel Collins, "Debat," *Dictionary of World Literature,* edited by Joseph T. Shipley (New York: The Philosophical Library, 1943), p. 148.

[10] James H. Hanford, "Debate of the Heart and Eye," *MLN,* XXVI (1911), 162.

it may be regarded as a natural expression of the genius of that period. Yet, while these centuries witnessed the greatest popularity of this form, the debate is represented intermittently to the end of the Middle Ages. Its "sudden emergence and great popularity were undoubtedly due to the interest throughout the schools in dialectic poetry and to the rise of the courtly vernacular, in which the form soon made its appearance."[11] The debate had thus a vigorous life, so vigorous, indeed, that it did not become an outmoded verse form till much later than the thirteenth century. It was known by a variety of names: *conflictus, certamen, contentio, disputatio, altercatio, estrif, plet,* and *desputisoun.* But in every case the essential element was the same: there was always a spirited contest in verse between two or more disputants, each of whom claimed supremacy for the views he expressed.

The basis for the controversy in *The Debate between the Body and the Soul* is the idea of the relative responsibility of the body and the soul for the soul's fate. The soul heaps violent abuse upon the body for having brought about its destruction by sin; the body meets this abusive outburst, overwhelming the soul with a scathing counter-attack that reveals its own rôle as that of a passive instrument. The soul in desperation tries to shift the responsibility to God, first, by accusing Him of having erred when He created human nature, and then by reminding Him of having promised His mercy with which He covered the sins of His creatures.

It was no part of the debate convention for the poet (in this instance, the dreamer who overheard the dispute) to reveal himself to the disputants. Nor was it necessary for any verdict to be given. But the poet in *The Debate* builds up the case of the relative responsibility in the soul's loss by expressly giving the pros and the cons of the question at issue and also by pronouncing the judgment implicitly, after the close of the debate, by means of a graphic

---

[11] Sister M. Emmanuel, *op. cit.,* p. 148.

delineation of the tournament and hunt in which more than a thousand hellhounds torture the soul on the hellward road (ll. 364-372).[12]

Like many writers of the Middle Ages the poet clothed his conception in the vesture of a dream. This concept of the poet as a dreamer is age-old. It was in a dream that the unlettered swineherd Cædmon sang his "Song of Creation," which marked the birth of English lyric poetry. The dream as a device for launching a story on its way has been said to have come widely into Europe through Macrobius, who commented on and issued Cicero's *Somnium Scipionis*, the only part of his lost work, *De Republica*, which has been preserved. Wilbur O. Sypherd has observed that a likely source for the convention may be the visions of hell, purgatory, and heaven, "many elements of which have seemingly been appropriated by the love poems."[13] That there is some truth in Sypherd's assertion will be borne out by the references to the presence of medieval vision material in *The Debate between the Body and the Soul*, as subsequent pages will reveal.

In the state of reverie and sleep the mind, Saint Thomas Aquinas declares, is oblivious of external objects because the senses are more or less closed to impressions from without, the action of the understanding and of the will is temporarily suspended, and the imagination is the dominating faculty.[14] It may be that either the conscious or the un-

---

[12] *The Debate between the Body and the Soul*, Laud text. From now on all the references will be made from the *Laud* text unless the "Auchinleck" is specified. The writer has studied the microfilm of the *Laud MS* at the Library of Congress, Washington, D.C., has compared it with the text and the emendations as printed in Emerson's *Middle English Reader*, a reprint of which appears in the Appendix of this dissertation for the convenience of the reader.

[13] *Studies in Chaucer's House of Fame* (London: The Camden Society, 1907), p. 23.

[14] *Quæstiones Disputatæ. De Malo, III, iii ad ix. Opera Omnia* (Paris: Vives, 1889), XIII, 385: "Quod rerum species vel similitudines non decernantur a rebus ipsis, contigit ex hoc quod vis altior, quæ judicare et discernere potest, ligatur.... Sic ergo cum offeruntur imaginariæ similitudines, inhæretur eis quasi rebus ipsis, nisi sit aliqua alia vis quæ

conscious recognition of the imagination as the dominant power in sleep is the first consideration that caused many poets to use the medium of a dream. The ordinary person cannot comprehend the vividness with which the poet in his waking state *sees* his images; he has himself, however, experienced something similar in sleep when the images of fancy are not subject to the corrections which the presentations of the senses are ever furnishing during waking life. Otto Rank believes that "the fact that we all dream and, in dreams, are all (in the fine comparison of Schopenhauer) poets of the stature of Dante or Shakespere is sufficient by itself to force to our notice the fact that we do not know what it is which allows a Dante or a Shakespere to do in waking life what we all, according to Schopenhauer, do in our sleep."[15] Frederick Prescott shares a like thought in his remark that there is a "comparatively clear distinction between ordinary thought and waking vision, but that there is no such line between waking vision and the vision of sleep; one blends so naturally with the other that it is often impossible to tell from the record of them which is which."[16] It is not surprising that the poet, realizing this, often throws his conception into the form of a dream.[17]

Furthermore, it is not only the objects and events of the memory that the imagination shows more vividly in dreams than in waking hours; it is the inclination of the mind in sleep also to objectivize all the impressions which it receives. The poetic imagination inclines also toward objectivizing abstract conceptions and describing them by personification. It is this concreteness of the imagination, this expressing of one thing in terms of another, that links

---

contradicat, puta sensus aut ratio. Si autem sit legata ratio, et sensus sopitus, inhæretur similitudinibus sicut ipsis rebus, ut in visiis dormientium accidit, et ita in phreneticis." See also Commentary on Aristotle's *De Somniis*, Lect. IV, XXIV, 319-321; and Frederick C. Prescott, *The Poetic Mind* (New York: The Macmillan Company, 1922), p. 17.

[15] *Art and Artist: Creative Urge and Personality Development* (New York: Tudor Publishing Company, 1932), p. 26.
[16] *Op. cit.*, p. 16.
[17] *Ibid.*, pp. 12-14.

dreams and poetry,[18] and makes it easy for the poet to express his imaginings under the semblance of a dream. The poet who is trying to see beyond the veil, to express eternal truths, will find an advantage in the possibility of ignoring the exigencies of time and space in a dream-poem. The human mind, it is true, is capable of imagining almost any set of circumstances on this side of the grave; yet it is quite unable to imagine conditions on the other side, simply because they are in the realm of the spirit. It is in this roomy dream structure that the fictitious quarrel between the personified abstractions of the Body and the Soul has its being.

GENERAL STRUCTURE OF THE DEBATE

In *The Debate between the Body and the Soul* it is the dreamer's voice,[19] which may or may not be that of the poet, that provides the narrative framework in which the debate begins and moves. But unlike the voices of dreamers in the poetry of the Middle Ages, who fall asleep at the beginning and awaken at the end, this voice is heard at intervals throughout the poem, as it frequently prefaces the speeches of the debaters — the personified Body and the Soul — with short narrative remarks that artistically link them; and as it becomes the control in the play-by-play account of the burlesque tournament and chase, when the intellectual conflict gives way to the physical contest in the lists on the road to hell. In this account the narrator's voice is interrupted by the intrusion of the voice of the Soul (ll. 443-456), as it blasphemes God for having created man,[20]

---

[18] *Ibid.*, pp. 16 ff. See also Michael J. Maher, S.J., *Psychology: Empirical and Rational* (New York: Longmans, Green and Company, 1923), pp. 176-178; Dom Thomas V. Moore, O.S.B., *Dynamic Psychology* (Philadelphia: J. B. Lippincott Company, 1924), p. 36.

[19] Reference to a "voice" in any speech is "a part of the meaning and a frame for the rest of the meaning for the interpretation of which it supplies an indispensable control." See J. Craig LaDrière, "Voice and Address," *Dictionary of World Literature*, p. 615.

[20] Cursing and blaspheming God for having created man appears in "The Vision of Clerk Ode's Man," *Jacob's Well*, edited by Arthur Brandeis (London: *EETS OS*, 115, 1900), p. 10.

and the yelling fiends (ll. 457-464) as they remind the Soul of its vain efforts to implore assistance of Jesus Christ and Mary now that its doom has been sealed.

The dreamer's voice is heard first as he sets the stage, simply and directly.[21]

>   Als I lay in a winteris nyȝt
>   In a droupening bifor þe day,
>   Forsoþe I sauȝ a selly syȝt,
>   A body on a bere lay,
>   Þat havede ben a mody knyȝt
>   And litel served God to pay;
>   Loren he haved þe lives lyȝt,
>   Þe gost was oute and scholde away. (ll. 1-8)

As is appropriate to the eerie vision of the dreamer, his inspiration possesses him at night. It is a winter's night before the day when he beholds the body bereft of the breath of life. The phrase, *bifor þe day*, represents the period before daybreak, which is the coldest time of the night since it is the hour furthest away from the time when the sun's rays have struck the earth. It is the time, too, when most of the heat that has been absorbed during the day has been given off by radiation. *Winter's night* is, therefore, a night that is cold and barren. The association of night and its darkness, or the absence of light, with winter and its coldness, or the absence of life, becomes almost symbolic of the sin that has darkened and damned the soul. The allusion to the narrator's own dejected mood is typical of that coupling of the phases of nature and human moods which became almost a convention in medieval literature.[22] With this economy of words the narrator prepares for the bier, for the cold desolate body from which has been extinguished the light that had

---

[21] Dr. Eleanor Henningham has pointed out that throughout its history the dialogue elements in the Body-and-Soul legend "always tended to grow at the expense of the setting." See footnote 27 in "Old English Predecessors of the *Worcester Fragments*," *PMLA*, LV (1940), 298.

[22] See *English Lyrics of the Thirteenth Century*, edited by Carleton Brown (Oxford: Clarendon Press, 1932), esp., pp. xiv and 14.

enkindled life, and for the Soul that stands nearby bewailing the sins of the body.

At the close the dreamer's voice is heard again in a tone of fright and fear that springs from the perception of what he has seen. He is overwhelmed at the sight:

> On ilk a her a drope stod
> For friȝt and fer þer as I lay;
> To Jesu Crist with milde mod
> Ʒerne I kalde and lokede ay,
> Ʒwan þo fendes hot and wod
> Come to fette me away. (ll. 475-480)

and rejoices at his own salvation from such a fate as befell the soul (ll. 481-484). He entreats the sinful soul to repent, because "Never was done sin so great that Christ's mercy is not well more" (ll. 487-488).

The situation above in lines 1-8 calls to mind the lines in Milton's *Comus:*

> Such are those thick and gloomy shadows damp
> Oft seen in charnel vaults and sepulchres,
> Lingering and sitting by a new-made grave,
> As loth to leave the body that it loved,
> And linked itself by carnal sensuality
> To a degenerate and degraded state.[23] (ll. 470-475)

and of Plato's *Phædo:*

> But, I think, if when it [soul] departs from the body it is defiled and impure, because it was always with the body and cared for it and loved it and was fascinated by it and its desires and pleasures, so that it thought nothing was true except the corporeal, which one can touch and see and drink and eat and employ in the pleasures of love and if it is accustomed to hate and fear and avoid that which is shadowy and invisible to the eyes but it is intelligible and tangible to philosophy — do you think a soul in this condition will depart pure and uncontaminated?... it will be interpenetrated I suppose, with the corporeal which intercourse and communion with the body have made a part of

---

[23] *The Works of John Milton,* edited by Frank Allen Patterson (New York: Columbia University Press, 1931), I, Part I, 102.

its nature because the body has been its constant companion and the object of its care.... And such a soul is weighed down by this and is dragged back into the visible world, through fear of the invisible and of the other world, and so, as they say, it flits about the monuments and tombs, where shadowy shapes of souls have been seen, figures of those souls which were not set free in purity but retain something of the visible; and this is why they are seen.[24]

The dreamer's voice designates the status of the deceased.

> A body on a bere lay,
> þat havede ben a mody knyȝt
> And litel served God to pay; (ll. 4-6)

This body had been a knight who was accorded high rank in society. As a member of the knightly class, it was expected that he possess the essential chivalric virtues which had always been a fundamental feature of knighthood. These included loyalty, lavish generosity or largesse, and courtesy or self-forgetfulness in the desire to be of service to others. The knight's main duty consisted in rendering unflinching loyalty to his lord, which must never fail him as God's fidelity never fails. To the feudal world loyalty meant the observance of mutual obligations which bound the members of the caste.

The knight in *The Debate between the Body and the Soul*, unlike the true and exemplary knight that stands at the entrance of the Canterbury gallery, fell far short of the chivalrous pattern. He had been a *mody knyȝt;* i.e., he was proud and haughty. It may be said that pride, the sin of the feudal and hierarchic age,[25] was his besetting sin, and as such was the source of the other deadly sins. He had undertaken worldly pursuits for worldly renown, and like the natural man who acts from natural motives

---

[24] *Phædo*, 80, edited by H. Fowler. Loeb Library. (New York: G. Putnam's Sons, 1929), I, 283-285.

[25] J. Huizinga, *The Waning of the Middle Ages* (London: E. Arnold and Company, 1924), p. 58.

only, he confined his thoughts and acts to the narrow sphere of his own interests and neglected to pay God the honor due to Him. "And litel served God to pay" (l. 6).

The knight's quest for adventure must necessarily be done on horseback. The horse and the horseman are utilized by the poet as a primary image that is rich in reference:

> þou þat were woned to ride
> Heyȝe on horse in and out,
> So kweynte kniȝt ikuþ so wide,
> As a lyun fers and proud, (ll. 17-20)

By means of this horse-and-rider image the threads of the chivalric matter and of the Body-and-Soul legend elements are skillfully interwoven. The glories and the splendors of knightly halls, of tournaments and the chase, and of the loves of ladies and of friends parallel the contrasting terror and gloom of the grave, the hideousness of the devils, and the writhing pains of the soul in hell.

Not unlike the knights of the medieval romances, the poet's knight has gained fame through his action and prowess at home and abroad. The stock figure in the lines above comparing the knight's skill in battle with that of a fierce and proud lion recurs again and again in medieval romances, and in vision literature the lion becomes emblematic of the temptations to which the knight is exposed from ambition.[26]

In the lines quoted above, it is plainly evident that the horse-and-rider image has little more than physical reference, that the relation between the horse and rider is solely

---

[26] Thomas Wright, *St. Patrick's Purgatory: An Essay on the Legends of Purgatory, Hell, and Paradise Current During the Middle Ages* (London: John Russell Smith, 1844), p. 123. See also A. Dante's *Inferno*, translated into English by Henry F. Cary (New York: P. F. Collier and Son, 1901), Canto I, where the panther, lion, and wolf are emblematic of temptations of sensuality, ambition, and avarice, respectively.

physical. Through the voice of the Soul the dreamer is merely endeavoring to show that the joy of the knights was in their strength and skill in battle, and in the hardiness and the beauty of their horses and their armor. But in the following lines

> ...Is no doute;
> Abouten, bodi, þou me bar;
> þou mostist nede, I was wiþoute
> Hand and fot, I was wel war. (ll. 161-164)

where the Soul states its reason for being borne about by the body, the relationship is more intimate and fundamental; the meaning becomes philosophical or psychological. The rider, that is, the soul, becomes the mover, and the horse, that is, the body, that which is moved. The contact between the soul and the body is conceived, then, not as an essential one, but as an accidental one. The soul is united to the body not as form is to matter but as a motor to a boat.

There is yet another meaning in these lines: if the reference is to the man-and-horse together, then the rider is understood to be in control of the horse. In that case the knight must be so ordered that his soul is always in control in the struggle between the law of the mind and the law of the members; and the dreamer, like most religious writers of the Middle Ages, was chiefly concerned, in his rôle as narrator, with the inner ordering and government of man.

This image of the rider and the horse is retained even in the elaborate allegory in the last seventeen stanzas where the soul is compelled by the demons to give a display of its earthly life, and this, in keeping with the idea of conflict and the spirit of knighthood, assumes the form of the tournament.

Within the narrative frame but a part of the fictive dialogue is a subsidiary structure of the *Ubi sunt?* type, a type of poem on the transience of life and fame, dating back to the time of the Old Testament.²⁷ The *Ubi sunt?* appeared among the ancients, became a commonplace in the Middle Ages,²⁸ and the medieval formula lingered on into modern times when it was made famous by François Villon, who

---

²⁷ Thomas Batiouchkof noticed the *Ubi sunt?* in Ephræm the Syrian (*Opera syr. et lat.*, III, p. 316) and in a Homily of Cyril of Alexandria. Batiouchkof thinks that the literary theme began with Ephræm: "Cyrille semble avoir emprunté à saint Ephrem cette façon de demontrer le neant des aspirations mondaines et la fragilité de la vie humaine." "Le Debat de l'Ame et du Corps," *Romania*, XX (Paris: 1891), 545, note 1. Etienne Gilson in *Idees et les lettres* (Paris: Librairie Philosophique de la Sorbonne, 1932), p. 13, shows that the *Ubi sunt?* in Ephræm and Cyril is a formula of St. Paul literally utilized. Gilson refers to the Epistle of St. Paul to the Corinthians, I, i: 19-20: "Where is the 'wise man'? Where is the scribe? Where is the disputant of this world? Has not God turned to foolishness the 'wisdom of this world?'" He finds the *Ubi sunt?* also in Isaias xxxiii: 18, and in Baruch iii: 16-19. (All New Testament quotations in English will be from the revision of the Challoner-Rheims Version, Patterson, New Jersey: St. Anthony Guild Press, 1941. Old Testament, from the Douay Version, New York: Douay Bible House, 1941.)

²⁸ The *Ubi sunt?* motif is of frequent occurrence in homilies. Eleanor Kellogg Henningham has pointed out that the Vercelli homilist has worked the motif into the speech of the soul in the Fourth Homily. See Max Förster *Die Vercelli Homilien, Bibliothek der Angelsächsischen Prosa*, XII (Hamburg, 1932), 98. This is the only homily she found in any language that makes this theme an actual part of the Soul's speech. See "Old English Precursors of the *Worcester Fragments*," 229, note 32. The *Ubi sunt?* appears also in the following homilies but not as a part of the Soul's dialogue: Corpus Christi College, Cambridge *MS 201*, printed by Benjamin Thorpe, *Ancient Laws and Institutes of England*, folio edition (London: G. E. Eyre and A. Spottiswoode, 1849), pp. 466 ff.; *MS Junius 85*, p. 410 [This section of the MS has not been printed by Professor Willard; the first part appeared in "Address of the Soul to the Body," *PMLA*, L (1935), 961 ff.]; in Blickling Homily VIIIa in *The Blickling Homilies of the Tenth Century*, edited by Richard Morris (London: *EETS OS*, 58, 1874), p. 97, based on a passage in No. 58 of the *Sermones ad Fratres in Eremo* (printed in Migne, *PL*, XL, 1341); in Homily XII in *Twelfth Century Homilies*, edited by A. O. Belfour, Part I (London: *EETS OS*, 137, 1909), 131 ff. For the motif elsewhere in Old English literature, see F. Kluge, "Zu Altenglischen Dichtungen, 2. Nochmals der Seefahrer," *Englische Studien*, VIII (1885), 472 ff. See also *Early Latin Debate of the Body and the Soul*. Preserved in *MS Royal 7 A III* in the British Museum, edited by Eleanor Henningham, Ph.D. Dissertation of the University of New York (New York: Published privately, 1939), p. 45, for a parallel study of the *Ubi sunt?* in *þe Desputisoun bitwen þe Bodi and þe Soule*, the French *Un Samedi par Nuit*, and the *Royal Debate*.

gave it soft tenderness in "Mais ou sont le neiges d'antan?" There are, however, many modern illustrations of the formula.[29]

While the *Ubi sunt?* was at one time an individual poem, the tendency is to place the query in the opening line of a stanza or to use it as a refrain or repetend. This *Ubi sunt?* section occupies twenty-eight lines in the *Laud* text[30] of *The Debate between the Body and the Soul*, and so dense are they with evocative realism that they give a complete picture of a luxurious life cut short by death. Appropriately, the speech is placed in the mouth of the Soul, since it is the body that delighted in luxurious living. The Soul reviews one by one the things of the world the knight valued most, what gave him his greatest delight, and how all these pleasures have nothing behind them and how worthless are worldly goods after death. The Soul describes little; it enumerates in the manner of a teacher who calls the roll of her pupils and there appear castles and towers (ll. 33-36), soft garments and rich palls (ll. 37-38), sumpters with their rich trappings, proud palfreys and steeds reminiscent of tournaments and jousts; falcons and hounds symbolic of hawking and hunting (ll. 25-30).

A deep impression is left on the reader's fantasy by this sober and austere speech of the Soul about a smiling world, a knightly world, in which pleasure appears in lordly castles, in the attractive chase, in jousts, in tournaments, in feast, and in song. Precisely because the evocation is so rapid there is felt all that is pathetic and passing and the rapid strokes of the poet suggest the rapidity with which everything passes in this world. But this transience of wealth and material glory is even more intensified by concluding each group of six lines of the eight-line stanzas with two lines relative to the present contrasting condition of the body, now that it has been bereft of the soul. The

---

[29] For a bibliography of the *Ubi sunt?* in literature, see Gilson, *Idees et les lettres*, pp. 31-38.

[30] In the "Auchinleck," "Vernon," *Digby*, and *Royal* texts it occupies more lines.

lines referring to the knightly bower are contrasted with two lines describing the dark bower in which the body will be placed in burial.

> Wreche, ful derk is nou þi bour;
> Tomoruwe þou schalt þerinne falle.³¹ (ll. 39-40)

And the body that has been accustomed to wear fine clothing has been stripped of its gear from head to foot and wrapped in a shroud.

> Ʒwi list ou þere so bare o side
> Ipricked in þat pore schroud? (ll. 23-24)

The foul flesh that has steeped itself in gluttony in its lifetime is now consigned to the loathsome pit where foul worms shall mangle it.

> To do þat foule fleys to swelle
> þat foule wormes scholden ete? (ll. 45-46)

Gluttony has merited for the Soul the pains of hell.

> And þou havest þe pine of helle
> With glotonye me bigete. (ll. 47-48)

Unlike its speech in the "Old English Address" and in the *Worcester Fragments* the Soul does not tell with appalling realism the first coming of the worms³² to the grave

---

³¹ Compare the lines in *Erthe Upon Erthe*, edited by Hilda M. R. Murray (London: *EETS OS*, 141, 1911), "Erþ bilt castles, and erþe bilt toures, Whan erd is on erþe, blak beþ þe boures," p. xxx.

³² Both the "Old English Address" and the *Worcester Fragments* contain elaborate descriptions of the destruction of the body by worms. The best edition of "Old English Address" appears in *The Vercelli Book, The Anglo-Saxon Poetic Records*, II, edited by George Philip Krapp (New York: Columbia University Press, 1932), 54-59. The most convenient edition of the *Worcester Fragments* is that by Richard Buchholz, *Die Fragmente der Reden der Seele an den Leichnam, Erlanger Beiträge*, Bd. I (1890), Hft. VI. Direct references to the body's becoming food for worms appear frequently in the *memento-mori* sermons. See Wulfstan's Homily XXX, p. 149, in A. S. Napier (ed.), *Wulfstan, Sammlung der ihm zugeschriebenen Homilien nebst Untersuchungen über ihre Echtheit* (Berlin: Weidmann, 1883); in Blickling

and the fearful destruction wrought, for *The Debate*, in contrast with these pieces, places emphasis upon the soul's tortures in hell, not on the disintegration of the body.

For perfect integration of the theme the poet reverts to the three types of pleasures — hunting and hawking, love of the lady, and friendship — in which the knight delighted. By means of these the poet shows the effect the knight's death has on the world. Through the voice of the Soul come intimations that the body loved hunting and hawking. The Soul does not directly assert that the Body loved these sports, but implies that it did by showing the effect of the knight's death on beasts and fowls, which may now roam freely and lie at ease under trees.

> Nou mouwe þe wilde bestes renne
> And lien under linde and lef,
> And foules flie bi feld and fenne,
> Siþin þi false herte clef. (ll. 113-116)

Hunting and hawking were the chief sports of the gentry. Hunting was then what English fox-hunting is today, a social affair, but it included among its devotees many more strata of society and filled a larger social need than at the present day. The *wilde bestes* are the four "beasts of the chase" — buck, doe, martin, fox, roe — as distinct from the "beasts of the forest" or of "venery" — hind, hart, boar, wolf.[33] Distinctions between these classes were vague. "Beasts of the chase" were found living in royal forests[34] as well as "beasts of venery." Henry Savage has already

---

Homily VIIIa, *op. cit.*, p. 99; in "De Sancte Andrea," in *Old English Homilies of the Twelfth Century*, edited by Richard Morris (London: EETS ES, 53, 1873), p. 182; Vercelli Homily IV, *Die Vercelli Homilien*, pp. 92 ff.

[33] Dame Juliana Berners, *The Boke of St. Albans* (London: Eliot Stock, 1901), Recto e¹.

[34] An English royal forest and those who dwelt in it were under the jurisdiction of the Law of the Forest. Anyone entering the area of the Forest to "squat," poach, or even to collect faggots without permission could be arraigned before a royal justice. For a brief treatment of Forest Law, see *Encyclopedia Britannica*, Eleventh Edition, XI, 644-645. For a more detailed account, consult *Select Pleas of the Forest*, edited by G. J. Turner (London: Selden Society, 1901), XIII.

remarked that terms meant "no more than the fact that certain animals were hunted in one way" and others in another and that the illegal slaughter of a "beast of the forest" brought a severer legal penalty than the slaying of a "beast of the chase," because "beasts of the forest" occupied a higher hunting category.[35]

There is yet another pleasure that the Soul concentrates upon in its speech to the Body, and one wonders what possible bond there is between the deadliness of vices and the daintiness of amorous fancies. These two conventions, one born of Gregory and the Fathers and the other of Ovid and the troubadours, blend in letters as well as in life. And here, too, is courtly love.

> Ne nis no levedi briȝt on ble,
>   þat wel were woned of þe to lete,
> þat wolde lye a niȝt bi þe
>   For nouȝt þat men miȝte hem bihete. (ll. 121-124)

The poet declares that in the knight's present condition no woman of bright complexion who had at one time rated his love high would now spend a night with him.

It appears as though the allusion to love in the lines quoted above is not love on the troubadour model, but love as the courtly writers of northern France took over the ideas of the troubadours and modified them to suit themselves. It was actually among the troubadours of southern France in the twelfth century that the "Ovidian material combined with other elements and this whole combination as it developed in the south" and spread over other lands produced what is now known as courtly love.[36] When the thirteenth-century poet

---

[35] "Hunting in the Middle Ages," *Speculum*, VIII (1933), 33.

[36] *Art of Courtly Love* by Andreas Capellanus, with Introduction, Translation, and Notes by John J. Parry (New York: Columbia University Press, 1941), p. 6. See also W. P. Ker, *Epic and Romance: Essays on Medieval Literature* (London: Macmillan, 1931), pp. 345-346. In referring to the Provençal element in the latter romances of northern France, W. P. Ker remarks of the Provençal lyric that "among the definite influences that can be proved and explained, one of the strongest is that of Latin poetry, particularly the *Art of Love*. About this can be no doubt, however great may seem to be the interval between the ideas of Ovid and those of the Provençal lyrists...."

sang of love, he was no longer aware of any distinction between the love of the Ovidian type and of the courtly love type. When the two concepts merged into one, the distinction became dull.³⁷ A knight was considered a better knight if he loved. Eleanor of Aquitaine brought it about that any man of fashion had to be in love or in battle, "for the best lovers make the best knights." ³⁸ The lover was regulated by principles ingeniously deduced and compiled under Eleanor of Aquitaine and Marie of Champagne.³⁹

It may be expected that the poet, in view of the importance that the Church attached to the things of the spirit and the life hereafter, which was his ultimate concern, would place this accusation against the Body in the mouth of the Soul; for the love of the knight for the lady, a primary and variable motive, is nothing other than sensuality transformed into the craving of self-sacrifice, into the desire of the male to show his courage, to incur danger, to be strong, to suffer, and to bleed. The contrasting motive, the hideousness of the Body, now that the Soul is out of it, makes it unsightly and uncomely for either the lady or the friend.

> þou art unsemly for to se,
>   Uncomli for to kissen swete;
> þou ne havest frend þat ne wolde fle,
>   Come þou stertlinde in þe strete. (ll. 125-128)

The Soul's allusion here may be to the concept of friendship, which, as a system of thought, might have clashed with the concept of courtly love. It is a truism that in the glorification of woman that was part and whole of courtly love there

---

³⁷ Urban T. Holmes, *A History of Old French Literature* (New York: F. S. Crofts, 1937), p. 313. Thomas A. Kirby [*Chaucer's Troilus: A Study in Courtly Love* (University: Louisiana State University Press, 1940), p. 4] says that the "great body of medieval love poetry is, in many respects, essentially Ovidian."

³⁸ Lu Emily Pearson, *Elizabethan Love Conventions* (Berkeley: University of California Press, 1933), p. 16.

³⁹ See Parry, *op. cit.*, pp. 13-21.

The General Character

entered a new rival of friendship. But unlike the ancients who exalted friendship, the medieval man did not lay enough stress on classical theories to make a conflict apparent. As the Churchmen of the Middle Ages made "friendship subservient to other worldliness, and as feudal conditions connected it with the virtues and the opposed vices of the feudal system, so courtly love thought friendship secondary to love."[40]

Great concreteness of detail is manifest in the last sixteen stanzas of *The Debate* which constitute the last part of the vision structure. The poet, through close adherence to his structural plan, transfers the quarrel from the "school room" to the open air, and the disputation becomes a "debate" in the sense of a physical conflict on the hellward road. The voices of the Body and Soul have been stilled, but the voice of the dreamer is heard as he gives his graphic account of the burlesque tournament[41] and the chase, in which the grotesque horror only heightens the feeling of pity and fear that the desperate recriminations of the Body and the Soul have produced. The Soul which had long severed its allegiance to Christ and had become steeped in the devil's lore (ll. 461-462) receives its just recompense (ll. 463-464).

---

[40] Lawrens Mills, *One Soul in Bodies Twain* (Bloomington: Principia Press, 1937), pp. 51-52.

[41] The tournament is reminiscent of the knight's performance in the infernal pageant of the *Vision of Thurcill* [E. K. Becker, *A Contribution to the Comparative Study of the Medieval Visions of Heaven and Hell, with Special Reference to Middle English Versions*. Ph.D. Dissertation of Johns Hopkins University (Baltimore: John Murphy, 1899), p. 97], as well as that in the "Dance of the Sevin Deidly Synnis," in *The Poems of William Dunbar*, edited by John Small (Edinburgh: Blackwood, 1893), II, 117-121. The Tartarus and Hades of ancient Greece "were sometimes moralized and burlesqued in the same manner as purgatory and hell of the Middle Ages. Among the philosophers of antiquity, and more especially among those of the Platonic school," there are infrequent allegorical descriptions of the regions of the shades. There may be mentioned, in Plato himself, the accounts of the infernal judges at the end of the *Gorgias*, of Tartarus in the *Phædo*, and of the vision of Er the Armenian in *The Republic*. Thomas Wright has referred to these in *St. Patrick's Purgatory*, p. 114.

It enters the lists with a host of more than a thousand devils,[42] who will haul it off to hell. There is a parallel here between the fiends who break in upon the scene with a bound, and the knights, who, on the morning of the tournament, troop to the listed plain, with the lords, ladies, and damsels, mounted on steeds and palfreys whose housings swept the ground. These devils are terrifying spectacles; they are hideous creatures, foul in their very aspect, blacker than pitch, with "brode bulches on here bac" and ragged and rough and tailed. Convinced of the existence of the devils, the medieval mind clothed them in every kind of deformity.

> In abreken at a breid
> A þousend develene and ȝet mo.
> . . . . . .
> For thei weren ragged, roue and tayled,
> With brode bulches on here bac; (ll. 363-364 and 369-370)

They are followed by the lord of shades, the Archfiend, or their master. The poet deviates from the regular vision devil and does not portray him as the "black gigantic man," immensely "broad and thick" and with claws of iron as he appears on the *Vision of Tundale*.[43] Nor was it necessary to describe him, because, being such a familiar character in

---

[42] See Apocalypse of St. Paul where ten thousand devils and more torment the souls of the damned with awls. It may be assumed that the influence of Vision writings is clear here. Louise Dudley, in the *Egyptian Elements in the Legend of the Body and Soul*, Bryn Mawr College Monographs (Baltimore: Furst, 1911), No. 8, p. 114, felt that the Middle English debate had lost the interesting distinction of the *Noctis sub Silencio Tempore Brumali* or the *Visio Fulberti*, printed by Thomas Wright, *The Latin Poems Commonly attributed to Walter Mapes*, pp. 95 ff., between the two demons that come for the soul and the many who torture it on the way to hell.

[43] Compare W. B. Turnbull, *The Vision of Tundale*, edited by Thomas Stevenson (Edinburgh: 87 Princes Street, 1843): "His body was bothe brood and thykke/ And as blakke as euer was pykke/....His nayles semyd of yron strong/ Full scharpe they were and full long" (ll. 1332-1333; 1350-1351).

medieval religious lore, he frequently acquired a stereotyped form. He is prince, not because of his power, but because his punishment is the prime punishment of all.[44] He leads the group in inflicting tortures of heat by smiting the Soul's heart with a white-hot colter.

> A devil kam þer atte laste
> þat was maister, wel I wot;
> A colter glowende in him he þraste
> þat it þoruȝ þe herte smot. (ll. 381-384)

Other devils transfix back and sides with white-hot swordblades, the points of which meet within, causing such gaping wounds that there appears on the body not a single spot where no blade strikes.

> Gleyves glowende some setten
> To bac and brest and boþe sides,
> þat in his herte þe poyntes mettin,
> And maden him þo woundes wide. (ll. 385-388)

There is implication here of the characteristic Christian feature that a suitable punishment was meted out for every crime.[45] The knight's besetting sin was pride and the devils are indirectly quoted in the dreamer's voice as saying this is the torture for his pride (ll. 389-390).

A group of devils lay their "scharpe long cloches" on the Soul, pull it about and toss it to and fro (ll. 365-368). Others tear the jaws asunder and pour hot lead into the mouth, bid the Soul to drink it, and then pour the surplus about it (ll. 377-379). This may have been a punishment inflicted for gluttony, as appears commonly in medieval

---

[44] See Thomas Wright, *St. Patrick's Purgatory*, p. 36.

[45] In the Apocalypse of St. Peter various sinners are tormented in accordance with the nature of their sins. This appears in Appendix 1 of *Religious Visions: The Development of the Eschatological Elements in Medieval English Religious Literature* (Amsterdam: H. J. Paris, 1932), by Arnold Van Os.

visions.⁴⁶ The agonized Soul writhes in pain and cries for mercy:

> ...Jesu, that sittest on hey,
> On me, þi schap, nou have merci.
> Ne schope þou me þat art so sly3?
> þi creature al so was I
> Als man þat sittes þe so ny3,
> þat þou havest so wel don by. (ll. 443-448)

It laments its doom and even insinuates that God was unjust in creating a hopeless creature like man. But its pleas are of no avail, for the period of mercy has ended and the time of justice is at hand. The theology of this particular passage is questionable. It is a part of Catholic belief, Saint Thomas declares, that the reprobate spirit, either human or angelic, has a will that is eternally and unchangeably dislocated, a will that is incapable intrinsically of repentance, of moral rectitude. It would be a most uncatholic presentation of hell to depict it as peopled with spirits that cry for mercy and come to find it. Time for mercy is past, chiefly because the lost spirit does not want mercy.⁴⁷ Instead of solace from God the fiends break the silence and for the first time they enter yelling, and with shrill voices they taunt the Soul:

> Caitif, helpeþ þe na more
> To calle on Jesus ne Marie,
> Ne to crie Cristes ore.
> Loren þou havest the cumpainye, (ll. 458-461)

The fiends remind the Soul that it is useless to call on Christ or Mary, since it has lost such company through sin.

On Judgment Day Jesus is to appear as the strict executor of justice and vengeance, and only an all-powerful mediator can incline Him to mercy. This mediator is the Blessed

---

⁴⁶ See the "Vision of Clerk Ode's Man," *Jacob's Well, loc. cit.*, where a glutton and drunkard was made to drink molten metal.

⁴⁷ *Summa Theologica*, Iᵃ, LXIV, ii; IIIᵃ "*Supplementum*," XCVIII, i, iii.

Virgin, who had earned the title *Mater Misericordiæ*, Mother of Mercy, because of her many miraculous interventions in favor of those who called upon her name in trouble or professed a particular devotion to her service. The medieval mind firmly believed that Mary's power of intercession would be exercised on behalf of man before the judgment seat of her Son, who could refuse no request when it was urged by His Mother. In the last stanza of the thirteenth-century lyric, "Doomsday," the voice of the speaker advocates prayer to Our Lady that she intercede for souls on the latemost day as they fare over the world.[48]

The sufferings inflicted by the demons, as discussed above, are preliminary to the clothing of the Soul for the tournament proper, in which the devils make sport of it by parodying its lot on earth. The victim is equipped with hell-attire, wearing the devil's coat of mail, which is white with heat and laced snugly to back and breast with "hote haspes" (ll. 393-398). A helmet, too, is added, before the Soul is made to ride away on a flaming charger.

>   An helm þat was litel to here
>   Kam him, and an hors al prest.

>   Forth was brouʒt þerewith a bridel,
>   A corsed devel als a cote,
>   þat grisliche grennede and ʒenede wide,
>   þe leyʒe it lemede of his þrote;
>   With a sadel to the midside
>   Fol of scharpe pikes schote,
>   Alse an hechele on to ride;
>   Al was glowende, ilke a grote. (ll. 399-408)

---

[48] See Carleton Brown, *Lyrics of the Thirteenth Century*, p. 46: "Bidde we ure lauedi, swetest alre þinge,/ Þat heo ure erende beore to þen heuonkinge,/ For his holi nome & for hire herendinge,/ Þat heo ure sawle to heouerige bringe." The first stanza of "Latemest Day" is a completion of this stanza: "Þene latemeste dai, wenne we sulen farren/ vt of þisse worlde wid pine & wid care,/ Al so we hideir comen naket & bare,/ & of ure fule sunnen yewen onsuare," p. 46.

In the use of the cursed devil as a horse[49] on which the Soul rides a part of the way to hell, it may be assumed that the dreamer is continuing the horse-and-rider image, which, as was said earlier in this chapter, is one of the primary images of the poem. There is little doubt that it was suggested to him as a way in which to make sport of the soul by parodying its lot on earth. But the poet had a sense of form, and if he utilized the horse-and-rider image in which may be shown the relationship of the body and the soul in determining what man is and how he is ordered, he undoubtedly found the horse-motif in this passage but fitting to the harmonious development of the poem.

> An hundred devel on him dongen
> Her and þer þan he was hent;
> With hote speres þoruȝ was stongen,
> And wiþ oules al torent;
> At ilke dint þe sparkles sprongen
> As of a brond þat were forbrent. (ll. 411-416)

As the Soul is made to run its course, a hundred demons assault it on every side, dragging it hither and thither, and thrusting white-hot spears into its flesh and tearing it with

---

[49] John de Bromyard [*Summa Prædicantium* (Basle: John of Amorbach, 1487), I, "Adulterium," v] in one of his graphic dilations, depicts the sinner as a horseman galloping to hell from stage to stage of the journey of Life; and the Vices are his steeds. See also the *Vision of Thurcill*, where a knight, who had spent his life in slaughter and rapine, is clad in armor and rides a black horse that emits flames and smoke from its mouth and nostrils. This miserable soldier, too, fixed to a saddle with long burning nails, is forced to suffer wretchedly under the weight and heat of his burning suit of armor. E. Becker, *op. cit.*, p. 97. There is, however, no specific connection with the way to the other world. While admitting that the two traits, the coat which the devils put on the soul, and the horse on which it rides part of the way to hell, were original with the Debate-poet, Louise Dudley supposes that the suggestion came from some other ideas about the soul with which he was familiar. The treatment is original so far as she knows. But for the motives she thinks he may have had suggestions. With regard to the motive of the horse, she calls attention to the vision of Pachomius and to the Pisentos story, in which the evil soul is taken to hell on a black horse; in the former it is tied behind the horse, and in the latter under it. It may have been suggested by the black horse that the demons sometimes ride when they take the soul. *Op. cit.*, p. 127.

awls. With each sting of the spear the sparks leap forth as from blazing firebrands that have been consumed by fire. In the above lines it appears as though the fiends assault the Soul with blazing brands, and as they do this the sparks fly as they do from a brand that has already been burnt up.

It appears as though the dreamer chose to describe the soul in concrete form; the representation given to the soul in the Old French debate was that of an infant. Thomas Batiouchkof[50] and Louise Dudley[51] have already pointed out that this conception is at the root of all versions of the Body and Soul legend. The soul had the form, if not of an infant, at least of a human being. This conception was popular in the Middle Ages. The soul is frequently pictured in human form in manuscript illuminations.[52] With this in mind it is easily believable that the Soul, which had been torn and mangled beyond the possibility of recognition, should again undertake its original shape to undergo new torments. In these passages quoted above the Soul has been torn by glowing blades, but it is about to endure more. This circumstance is constantly emphasized in Christian visions.[53]

The physical torments the devils have inflicted are twofold: there is, of course, the heat; there is always fire in hell; souls burn and bake. But unlike most Anglo-Saxon

---

[50] *Op. cit.*, pp. 517-518.

[51] *Op. cit.*, pp. 126-127.

[52] See Adolphe N. Didron, *Christian Iconography* or *The History of Christian Art in the Middle Ages*, translated by J. W. Millington (London: George Bell and Sons, 1886), I, 209-210, where there appears a plate depicting the hand of God holding souls in human form. The author comments thus: "In short, all the numerous texts contained in the Old and New Testaments seem to be condensed into one motive so often adopted among Greek Christians, and which represents the souls of the just, little naked human beings, praying with joined hands in the great hand of God; this hand issues from the clouds, whence it appears to have descended to earth to take the souls of the righteous, and return them to paradise."

[53] See W. B. Turnbull, *The Vision of Tundale*, p. 26, where Tundale, being delivered by the guiding of an angel to the fury of the fiend, is hewn into "gobettes smale." "He myght not dye for that peyn/ For he was sone hole ageyn" (ll. 783-784).

poets and Middle English vision writers, whose indignation takes delight in torturing their reprobates by a combination of contrasting heat and cold, the Debate-poet uses only heat. There is a second torment where souls are clawed by devils with flesh-hooks and with awls.[54]

After the Soul has run its course, it is unhorsed as in a tournament and driven to play the part of a quarry in the chase, a sport in which it had found diversion in its lifetime.

> ʒwan he hadde riden þat rode
>   Upon þe sadil þer he was set,
> He was kast doun as a tode,
>   And hellehoundes to him were let
> þat broiden out þo peces brode,
>   Als he to helle ward was fet;
> Ther alle þe fendes fet it trode,
>   Men miʒte of blod foluwe þe tred. (ll. 417-424)

In this hellward race the Soul is cast from the horse and forced to move on all fours like a toad, with a pack of hellhounds[55] turned loose upon it. Normal hunting excluded the fox,[56] which was looked upon as vermin and classed with the wild cats and wolves. But the dreamer compares the Soul to a toad, one of the group of vermin and voracious beasts, such as worms, snakes, scorpions, and dragon dogs, which tortured the inhabitants of hell.[57]

As the hellhounds and their quarry speed on their way the Soul is bidden to hunt and to blow the horn as a signal for Bauston and Bewis, its two hunting dogs that were so familiar with its calls.

---

[54] Devils with hooks appear in *Vision of Tundale* (ll. 371-372; 720 ff.; 1075, 1187).

[55] The devil appears as a hunter in the homily, "Sermo on Psalm CXIX," in *Old English Homilies of the Twelfth Century*, 53, p. 209.

[56] See *The Master of Game, The Oldest English Book on Hunting*, by Edward the Second, edited by William A. and F. Baillie-Grohman (New York: Ballantyne and Hanson, 1909), p. 213. In medieval hunting the fox was accounted a false beast, malicious as a wolf, and any means by which his death could be encompassed were considered legitimate, his extermination being the chief object in hunting him, not the sport.

[57] Van Os, *op. cit.*, pp. 19-20.

The General Character

> He beden him honten and blowen,
> Crien on Bauston and Bewis,
> þe ratches þat him were woned to knowen
> He scholden sone blowe þe pris; (ll. 425-428)

In these several lines the dreamer has bound together compactly the allusions to one of the most important matters of hunting technique — that governing music. All successful hunting music depends, in the last analysis, upon the training of the hounds, the coöperation of the hunters, and upon their thorough acquaintance with the task. It is assumed that in this burlesque hunt, as in any hunt, the hounds have a tendency to scatter, and they can be kept together only by the hunting music with which they are familiar. After the death of the quarry two *bays* were held, the one occurring early in the process of cutting and the other after having separated the head from the shoulders and flayed off the skin. At such times the *mort*[58] was blown, the hunters hallooed, and the hounds were encouraged to bay. When, in the opinion of the chief huntsman, baying had lasted long enough, the hounds were allowed a dole of meat — a necessity so that the discipline of the pack would not disintegrate.[59] But the music of the hunting horn was also used for the guidance of the hunters. If, as frequently happened, a hunter was lost, he indicated his distress by a note of *forlonge*[60] upon his bugle, and this brought from his more fortunate companions an answering note of *parfit*.[61]

In the lines above the Soul is compelled to *blowe* in order to signal that the game has been brought to bay and to raise a cry to the dogs that are to blow the *prise*.[62] The intermittent blowing of the *prise* informs the denizens of

---

[58] *Master of Game*, p. 175.
[59] *Ibid.*
[60] *Ibid.*, p. 173.
[61] *Ibid.*, p. 174.
[62] According to the *Master of Game*, p. 233, the *prise or coupling up* was to be blown by the chief personage of the hunt only after the quarry had been slain by strength or hunted, not when shot or coursed. The *prise* is a call consisting of four notes succeeded after a short interval (half an *Ave Maria*) by four notes a little longer than the first. *Ibid.*

hell of the successful day in that the quarry has been captured, and helps to bring back those who have been lost. At the response of the signal one hundred devils, in a row, draw the Soul with cords to the "loathly hole."

> An hundred develes, on a rowe,
>   With stringes him drowen, unþanc his,
> Til he kome to þat loþli lowe
>   Þer helle was, I wot to wis. (ll. 429-432)

This latter is, no doubt, an allusion to the second epistle of Saint Peter: "God spared not the angels that sinned, but delivered them drawn by internal ropes to the lower hell into torments."

The foul horde of fiends, after they have meted out a suitable punishment for every sin of the knight, catch the condemned soul by the head and tail and plunge it into hell.

> Þe foule fendes þat weren fayn,
>   Bi top and tail he slongen hit,
> And kesten it with myȝt and mayn
>   Doun into the develes pit, (ll. 465-468)

For the poet hell is in a definite place;[63] it is underground, a "devil's pit." The author designates hell by a

---

[63] In visions, hell and purgatory are sometimes depicted as being on the surface of the earth and the visitor walks around until he finds them in a remote valley. The more general notion, however, seems to have been that they were under the earth's surface and some writers have described exactly their position and extent. See *Pricke of Conscience*, edited by Richard Morris (Berlin: A. Ascher and Co., 1863), pp. 76-77: Þe stede, þat purgatory es calde,/ Under þe erthe es, als I halde,/ Aboven þe stede, als som clerkes telles,/ Þar crysom dede childer duells,/ Þat fra þe sight of Goddes face/ Er putted for ever, with-outen grace./ Þat place es neghest aboven hel pitte,/ Bytwen purgatory and itte./ Þus standes þe stede of purgatory,/ Oboven þam bothe in þat party (ll. 2787-2797)....Alle þir stedes men may helle call,/ For þai er closed with-in þe erthe alle (ll. 2816-2817). St. Augustine expresses the opinion that hell is under the earth. *Retractiones*, II, XXIV, n. 2; *PL*, XXXII, 640. On the ground of its name Gregory the Great sees no reason for not believing that hell is situated under the earth. He says that some hold hell is somewhere on the earth; others that it is under the earth. But he quickly hastens to add that he dare not decide the question. *Dials.*, IV, xlii; *PL*, LXXVII, 400.

number of words and phrases that echo medieval visions.[64] The words, *pit, abyss, well*, naturally carry with them the connotations of darkness. "þere sonne ne schal nevere be seyn" (l. 469). It may be said that darkness is so thick that it may be felt; and since the sun never shines, there is everlasting night. It is a land of horror where the wicked are tormented because they loved darkness rather than light.

To say that fire is the most striking phenomena of hell, where there is everlasting night, seems almost paradoxical. Perhaps that is the reason why the *Laud* text uses "pitch" in substitution for the "wild fir" in the "Auchinleck" text.

> þe erþe it openede anon,
>   Smoke and smoþer up it wel;
> Boþe of pich and of brimston,
>   Men myʒte fif mile have þe smel. *Laud* (ll. 435-438)

> The erþe opened and tochon,
>   Smoke and smorþer þerant welle,
> Of wild fir and of bronston
>   Seuen mile men miʒt have þe smelle. "Auch." (ll. 539-542)

Theodore Spencer[65] has already observed that in all medieval eschatologies fire was the chief means of punishment. It is emphasized in every medieval vision and in the works of the Fathers of the Church. It is flameless fire. Aelfric speaks of fires burning in swart darkness.[66]

---

[64] In practically all medieval visions hell is described as a pit. In "Chaucer's Hell: A Study in Medieval Conventions," *Speculum*, II (1927), 181, Theodore Spencer made the following observations: Drihthelm, in the seventh century, while in the other world, saw dusky flames rise from a great *pit* which was full of agonized souls. Tundale saw hell as a pit; and the phrase, "pit of helle," is a favorite one with the English author of *St. Patrick's Purgatory* [*Early South English Legendary*, edited by Carl Horstman (London: *EETS OS*, 87, 1887)], where in twenty lines (vv. 357-377) hell is spoken of eight times as a "pit."

[65] *Op. cit.*, p. 190.

[66] See B. Thorpe, *The Homilies of the Anglo-Saxon Church* (Oxford: Published for the Aelfric Society, 1895), I, 133. "Þa earman forscyldegodan cwylmiaþ on ecum fyre, and swa-þeah þet swearte fyr him nane lihtinge ne deþ." See also p. 533: "Witodlice þaet hellice fyr haefþ unasecgendlice byrnþ on sweartum þeostrum."

Stench, too, is among the horrors of the dreamer's hell, but it cannot be agreed with Theodore Spencer that it was "left to the medieval imagination to add this feature."[67] Stench and filth were invariable attributes of patristic hell,[68] and visionary hell smelled strongly of burning pitch, sulphur, and brimstone[69] as does the hell of *The Debate*.

There are mental sufferings, too, which are implied in the line — þou hast lorn þi mikel bliss (l. 132). The "mikel bliss" is undoubtedly the Beatific Vision. The Fathers emphasize these mental tortures. One of the most striking torments the mind must undergo in hell is the exclusion of the sight of God. Victims must suffer in their understanding, for the Divine Light has no communication with infernal darkness. They suffer in their memory by recalling the unspeakable joys of heaven which they have sacrificed carelessly through pride. Finally, they suffer in their will, which is filled with envy, hatred, and resentment, to which are added the special pains of hell.

This investigation thus far reveals that the general structure of *The Debate between the Body and the Soul* consists of a narrative framework wedding the knightly and the ascetic ideal through the voice of the interlocutor who is the dreamer. Within this framework and welded to the entire structure is the fictitious quarrel heard

---

[67] *Op. cit.*, p. 191.

[68] See Becker, *op. cit.*, pp. 48-77, for a discussion of Anglo-Saxon hell and purgatory as revealed in vision literature.

[69] See "Vision of Drihthelm," Bede's *Ecclesiastical History of the English Nation*, translated by J. E. King. Loeb Library. (London: G. Putnam's Sons, 1930), II, v. 112; "St. Patrick's Purgatory" *(South English Legendary)*, 309-310; 357-358; 362-363; 376-379; 406-412; these stinking pits are in purgatory. In "XI Pains of Hell," 227-228 (a Middle English version of the Vision of St. Paul), *Old English Miscellany*, edited by Richard Morris (London: EETS OS, 49, 1872), the foul stench is strong enough to have slain every Christian man. "A Tretyse of gostly batayle," *Yorkshire Writers: Richard Rolle of Hampole and His Followers*, edited by Carl Horstman (New York: The Macmillan Company, 1896), II, 420, contains "hote ffyre brynnyng withoutyne lyghte, with brymstone most stynkyng."

through the voices of the personified abstractions of the Body and the Soul. Another structure, the *Ubi sunt?* motif, a subsidiary structure, becomes a part of the whole through integration in the leading speech of the Soul. A part of the debate as an implicit expression of judgment, but included in the organic whole through the voice of the dreamer, is the physical conflict on the road to hell. The poet, through close adherence to his structural plan, transfers the quarrel from the "school room" to the open air, and the disputation becomes a "debate" in the sense of a burlesque tournament and a hunt, sports in which the Soul delighted in its lifetime. The metaphor of the horse and the rider, which functions primarily in the debate, has three levels of reference — the physical, the psychological, and the ethical — a history of the nature of which will be discussed in the next section.

HISTORY OF THE HORSE AND RIDER IMAGE

The image of the horse and the horseman in which there is the implied comparison of the relationship existing between the body and the soul has had a long history and has appeared, in its present construction, in the writings of the Orient, of the Fathers of the Church, of the Greeks and the Romans, and in the prose and poetry of the Middle Ages.

Pseudo-Hermes Trismegistus, whose writings figure largely in the Middle Ages,[70] uses the image of the horse and the horseman in his treatise, *De Castigatione Animæ*. In this treatise Hermes, in recommending the mastery of the soul over the body, compares the soul to a horseman and the body to a horse. He declares that if the horse rules the horseman, both must inevitably rush to destruction.

---

[70] Maurice De Wulf, *History of Philosophy*, translated by P. Coffey (New York: Longmans, Green and Company, 1909), p. 72.

The same is true of the body and the soul if the body is left to rule the soul. Hermes writes: "Si equus equitem regat, necesse est ambo in perniciem incurrant; si denique corpus animam regat, necesse est ambo in perniciem incurrant."[71]

In his commentary on *De Castigatione Animæ*, Bardenhewer links the use of the rider and the horse explanation of the soul and the body with the name of Plato. "Similitudinem equitis et equi quod attinet, notum est Platonum, *Phædr.*, 246, totam animam coniuncta vi rectoris ad decorum equorum comparare."[72] When Socrates speaks to Phædrus of the nature of the soul, he declares that he will illustrate what he has to say by the use of a figure which will be that of the united strength of a winged chariot.[73]

Saint John Chrysostom also employs the horse-and-rider image in a like sense when, in speaking of the control of the soul over the body in *Homily XIII* of the Epistle of Saint Paul to the Romans, he declares that if one quenches the light, casts out the holder of the reins, and chases the helmsman away, then he must charge the tossing to himself.[74] In *Homily V* Saint Chrysostom says that when the mind becomes undistinguishing, and the holder of the reins corrupted, all else is dragged out of course and overturned.[75]

Similarly, Philo the Jew interprets the horse and rider in Exodus iv: 1, where Moses and the children of Israel sing of the drowning of the horse and the rider. Philo supposes Moses means that God cast to utter ruin and the bottomless

---

[71] M. O. Bardenhewer, *Hermetis Trismegisti de castigatione animæ libellum* (Bonnæ: 1873), p. 105.

[72] *Ibid.*, p. 138.

[73] The figure as such does not actually appear in the *Dialogues* but may have been suggested by *Phædo*, 80, where the soul is the ruler and the guide of the body (See Plato, *Phædo*, 80, p. 279) and the *Phædrus*, 246, edited with English translation by H. Fowler. Loeb Library. (New York: G. Putnam's Sons, 1929), I, 471 ff.

[74] *PG*, XXVIII, 517: "Si vero tu lumen extinguas, et aurigam dejicias, gubernatoremque expellas, tibi postea tempestatem imputa."

[75] *Ibid.*, 421: "Postquam enim mens reproba facta est, auriga corrupto, omnia demum labefactantur et subvertuntur." (Plato, *Phædrus*, 246A)

abyss the four passions — grief, fear, desire, pleasure — and the wretched mind mounted on them. He draws a distinction, however, between the horseman and the rider, declaring that the "Horseman's business is to subdue his horse and to use the bit when he disregards the rein, whereas the rider's business is to be carried wherever the animal takes him."[76] The horseman who subdues the passions is not drowned, but dismounting from them, he awaits the salvation that comes from the master.[77] Philo also describes the actual conflict between the soul and the body in terms of the image of the horse and the rider and of the boat and the helmsman:

> Most profitless is it that the Mind should listen to Sense-perception, and not Sense-perception to the Mind; for it is always right that the superior should rule and the inferior be ruled; and Mind is superior to Sense-perception. When the charioteer is in command and guides the horses with the reins, the chariot goes the way he wishes, and if the horses have become unruly and got the upperhand, it has often happened that the charioteer has been dragged down and that the horses have been precipitated into the ditch by the violence of their motion, and that there is a general disaster. A ship, again, keeps her straight course, when the helmsman grasping the tiller steers accordingly, but capsizes when a contrary wind has sprung over the sea, and the surge has settled in it. Just so, when the Mind, the charioteer or the helmsman of the soul, rules the whole living being as the governor does a city, the life holds a straight course, but when the irrational sense gains the chief place, a terrible confusion overtakes it...[78]

Bardenhewer remarks that the comparison of the body to a ship directed by the soul, the helmsman, which is akin to the horse-and-rider metaphor, was also one of the most

---

[76] Philo (Judæus), *Works*, edited by F. H. Colson and G. H. Whitaker. Loeb Library. (New York: G. Putnam's Sons, 1929), I, II, 26, 289.
[77] *Ibid.*
[78] *Ibid.*, III, 79, p. 453.

common figures of the Platonists.[79] He shows further in his commentary on *De Castigatione Animæ* that Aristotle had already discussed the meaning of that comparison and had found it misleading.[80]

Bardenhewer also makes the observation that Plotinus found that comparison incorrect in his *Enneads*.

Of the modes currently accepted for the presence of one thing in another, none really meets the case of the soul's relation to the body. Thus we are given as a parallel the steersman in a ship; this serves adequately to indicate that the soul is potentially separable, but the mode of presence, which is what we are seeking, it does not exhibit.

We can image it within the body in some incidental way — for example, as a voyager in a ship — but scarcely as a steersman: and, of course, too, the steersman is not omnipresent to the ship as the soul is to the body... Is it any help to adopt the illustration of the steersman taking the helm, and to station the soul within the body as a steersman may be thought to be within the material instrument through which he works? Soul, whenever and wherever it chooses to operate, does in much that way move the body.

---

[79] Plato had said that the soul is in the body as a sailor in a boat. *De Anima*, I, 13. St. Albert the Great held the same point of view. See Book II, *De Anima*, I, 4, *Opera Omnia*, edited by A. Borgnet (Paris: Vives, 1890-1899), V, 198-199. This image is employed also in the Old French debate of the body and the soul, the *Un Samedi par Nuit*, ll. 803 ff. The best edition is that of Hermann Varnhagen [Erlanger Beiträge, I (1889), Part I, Appendix I, 114-196]. It is also found in the treatise of Hildebert, *De querimonia et conflictu spiritus et carnis*, in which there is a dialogue between the body and the soul told in the form of a vision. See Jacob Hommey, *Supplementum patrum* (Paris: 1864), pp. 421-440; *PL*, CLXXI, 989-1004; *Dictionaire des legendes*, 1080, declares that the work entitled *De quærimonia* is inserted in the works of St. Hildebert, although it is not certain that this saint is the author of the production, in mixed verse and prose. Dupin in *Bibliotheque des auteurs ecclesiastiques* attributes it to Hugh, bishop of Lyons, who died in 1106. However, *Histoire Litterature de la France*, XI, 357-359, says: "We do not find any literary work under this title, nor any which comes near to it in the ancient manuscript of the *Corbie*, which contains the writings or the works of Hugh Foulois." The editor of the works of Hildebert does not assert that this prelate or Hugh would be the author. This last observation was made by Batiouchkof, *op. cit.*, p. 565, note 1.

[80] Bardenhewer, *op. cit.*, p. 127. See also Aristotle, *De Anima*, edited by W. S. Hett. Loeb Library. (Cambridge: Harvard University Press, 1935), I, Book I, III, 406a, 5-10; Book II, I, 413a 5-10.

No; even in this parallel we have no explanation of the mode of presence within the instrument; we cannot be satisfied without further search, a closer approach.[81]

In his refutation of Colotes, the Epicurean, Plutarch also employs the horse-and-rider image to express the notion of relationship between the soul and the body. Colotes had evidently scoffed at Socrates for seeking to know what man is, and Plutarch says that Socrates was not a fool for searching himself, but those who undertake to investigate other knowledge first are fools, since the knowledge of self is so necessary and hard to find.

But let us ask Colotes, he says, how it is that man cannot continue living when he happens to reason with himself this way: "Come, what is this that I happen to be? Am I made up of a body and soul mixed, or does the soul use the body as a horseman uses his horse, without the two being a mixture of the horse and the man? Or are we each most authoritative in that part of the soul with which we think and reason and act, and are all the other parts of the soul and body instruments of this power? Or is there no essence to the soul at all, but is the body itself a mixture with the power of knowing and living?...These are the dreadful and perplexing questions in the *Phædrus*...[82]

Saint Augustine in *De Civitate Dei* speaks of this relation also. Varro, following the footsteps of Plato, decided that man was a nature made up of two things, body and soul. He knew that the soul was much better, but he doubted that it should be thought that man is simply a soul related to the body as a rider is to a horse. Rather, Varro considered the whole man to be body and soul together.[83] Saint Augustine commends Varro for holding that man is not soul alone, nor body alone, but both soul and body.[84]

---

[81] Plotinus, *On the Nature of the Soul, Being the Fourth Ennead*, translated from the Greek by Stephen McKenna (Boston: The Medici Society, Limited, 1924), III, 3, 21.
[82] Plutarch ad Coloten, c. 21, *Moralia*, edited by G. N. Bernardakis (Leipzig: B. G. Teubner, 1896), VII, Book XIV.
[83] XIX, 3; II, 404a; *PL*, XLI, 626.
[84] *Ibid.*

Again, the metaphor occurs in *De Moribus Ecclesiæ*, I, where Saint Augustine, concerned with the problem of what is more perfect than man, posits the question: "Is man soul and body as in the case of a team of horses or a centaur? Or is man nothing other than what we call the soul, though we so call it because of the body that it rules? For example, when we speak of a rider, the reference is not to the man and the horse together but to man alone..."[85] Saint Augustine is not in doubt as to whether man is only the rider which is the soul.

The image appears also in a passage in *De Ordine*, II, in a discussion of the relation of the soul to the body where Saint Augustine declares that the mind of the wise man remains immovable with Him. In the dialogue the voice *I* (and it may be assumed this is the voice of Saint Augustine) says, "But neither is the rider on the horse in such a manner that the horse holds empire over him; and although he drives the horse where he wants to go, yet when the horse is moved, it must be that the rider is moved."[86]

In medieval religious literature the relating of the body to a horse and the soul to a rider becomes a commonplace. Sister Mary Philippa[87] recognized the use of the metaphor in the body-soul context of the moral play, *Mankind*, where emphasis rests upon the responsibility of the rider to guide the horse:

> If a man haue an horse, and kepe hym not to hye,
> He may then reull hym at hys own dysere:
> Yf he be fede ouer well he wyll dysobey,
> And in happe caste his master in the myre.[88]

and in a Lenten sermon, where the body of man is likened to a horse:

---

[85] 4, 6; *PL*, XXXII, 1313.
[86] 4, 18; *PL*, XXXII, 1003.
[87] *Op. cit.*, p. 29.
[88] Ll. 234-237, *Chief Pre-Shakespearean Dramas*, edited by Joseph Quincy Adams (Boston: Houghton Mifflin Company, 1924).

"And so, dere freendes, most vs feede oure horsis, *scilicet*, oure bodies, with lizt metis at this tyme, that we mowe rynne the better a-yeyns the devel..."[89]

"A tretyse of gostly batayle," at one time attributed to Richard Rolle, uses the image in like manner: "For mannes body ys...lykenede to an horse; for lyke as one horse welle-taughte beryth hys mastere over many peryllys and saueth hym for perysshyng, so the body welle-rewled bereth the soule ouer many peryllys off thys wrecched worlde. And lyke as ther longeth many thyngis to the horse thorow the whych hys mastere may sytte sadly and not falle..."[90]

From this study of the history of the use of the metaphor of the horse and the rider it is evident that its function has been twofold: authors have employed the image either to express the notion of the relationship existing between the soul and the body in terms of the essence of man or to show that the responsibility of controlling man's actions rests with the soul.

---

[89] *Speculum Sacerdotale*, edited by Edward Weatherly (London: EETS OS, 200, 1936), p. 57.
[90] *Yorkshire Writers. Richard Rolle of Hampole and His Followers*, p. 421.

CHAPTER II

THE PSYCHOLOGICAL MEANING OF THE ANALOGY

From a consideration of the general structure of *The Debate between the Body and the Soul* and the history of the horse-and-rider analogy, we turn now to an analysis of the image on the psychological level.

It is evident from the lines

>Loren he haved þe lives lyȝt,
>þe gost was oute and scholde away. *Laud* (ll. 7-8)

>Forlorn he had his liues liȝt;
>þe gost moued out and wald oway. "Auch." (ll. 7-8)

that body and soul were present in the knight who was a man. The question now is, what is man? Of these two is he soul alone or body alone? For although body and soul are two realities, neither one of them would be called man unless the other were present (the body would not be man without the soul, and the soul would not be man if the body were not animated by it). The question involved here is not whether the knight *was mover*, but which *part* of the knight was mover, which part "he was moved by."

In the metaphor, *life's light*, the *light* which the body had lost when the soul moved out may be identified with what the medieval mind understood to be *corporeity* or the *first corporeal form*. Robert Grosseteste, in the twelfth century, uses the term *light* to designate this *first corporeal form*.[1] In his view *light* or the *first corporeal form* is more

---

[1] See "De Luce" in L. Baur's *Die Philosophischen Werke des Robert Grosseteste, Beiträge zur Geschichte der Philosophie des Mittelalters,* IX (Muenster: i. W., Aschendorff, 1912), 51: "Formam primam corporalem quam quidam corporeitatem vocant, lucem esse arbitror." Maurice De Wulf [*History of Medieval Philosophy*, translated by E. C.

than the *form of corporeity,* the principle of extension; it is also the principle of activity. Every body, Grosseteste believes, has a motion or activity which is natural to it, because it proceeds from an intrinsic principle. The intrinsic principle from which this motion or activity proceeds must be the form, since matter is passive.[2] Grosseteste further declares that light is the instrument by which the soul comes in contact with the body and with the things of sense.[3]

When Grosseteste speaks of this *first corporeal form,* he introduces a conception that is strange in Aristotelian

---

Messenger, third English edition (New York: Longmans, Green and Company, 1935), II, 57-58] says the *"quidam* are the Parisian scholastics, such as Alexander of Hales, whose main metaphysical theory Robert Grosseteste adopts." In the observation of Rev. Leo W. Keeler, however, the reference here would seem to be to Philip the Chancellor, who was the first to use the *form of corporeity* in the technical sense in which it appears throughout "De Luce." This Philip, according to Father Keeler's thesis, was one of Grosseteste's teachers at Paris. See "Dependence of R. Grosseteste's *De Anima* on the *Summa* of Philip the Chancellor," *The New Scholasticism,* XI (1937), 218.

[2] "De Luce," in L. Baur, *op. cit.,* p. 51.

[3] *Hexæmeron,* folio 147r a. In this philosophical piece on the discussion of light, Grosseteste uses the pseudo-Augustinian treatise, *De Spiritu et Anima, PL,* XL, 779-831. See D. E. Sharp, *Franciscan Philosophy at Oxford in the Thirteenth Century* (Oxford: University Press, 1930), p. 28. In the view of Maurice De Wulf the twelfth century adopted the *De Spiritu et Anima* as its manual of psychology. See *Scholasticism Old and New,* translated by P. Coffey (London: Longmans, Green and Company, no date), p. 124. *De Spiritu et Anima* illustrates "the union of the soul and body by the comparison of the ship and the pilot, and infers the *juxtaposition* in man of the two substantial beings." See also Baumgartner, *Die philosophie des Alanus de Insulis, BGPM,* II, 4 (Muenster: Aschendorf, 1896), 102 ff., where Alanus, who summed up and systematized the intellectual work of four centuries, represents the human soul as an independent substance associated to the body through a sort of *connubium* or *copula maritalis,* which is wrought by the agency of a *spiritus physicus.* De Wulf declares that the thirteenth century accepted and handed on the theory of *spiritus physicus,* bequeathed from the Greeks to the Middle Ages; but the Middle Ages did not follow Alanus by making the *spiritus* a third factor acting as a connecting link between the soul and the body. The thirteenth century saw in the *spiritus* an emanation of the informing principle, "an agency which disposes brute matter for activities of organic life." *Scholasticism Old and New,* p. 125.

doctrine. There is implied in this concept the doctrine of plurality of forms,[4] for the soul is then not the *first* principle, the ultimate, immanent basis of life.

In the poem under discussion, then, since *light of life* may be identified with the *first corporeal form*, not with the soul, it may be argued that the soul was the principle by which the knight understood, not the principle by which he lived. The Body's own words bear testimony to this as the verse — "A witteles best as y was born"[5] — clearly indicates. But as Aristotle has observed, if something is the first principle by which we understand, this must be the form of the body.[6] And the intellect is that by which the soul understands;[7] therefore, it must be the form of the body, since the soul is the principle by which a man understands and lives.[8]

But for the poet the principle of this act of understanding, a principle which is the intellect, was not the form of the body as is implied in the line — "A witteles best as y was born" — and is further corroborated by the Body's statement:

> I scholde have ben dumb as a schep,
> Or as an ouwe or as a swyn (ll. 153-154)

The body, it is clear, received its life from some other form. Unless the soul were its animating principle,[9] actually the body could have no existence. The body, in this case, could not have been that of a sheep or an ox. It

---

[4] See "De Statu Causarum," Baur, *op. cit.*, p. 125, where Grosseteste develops fully the doctrine of plurality of forms.

[5] "Auchinleck MS" (l. 210). The *Laud MS* reads, "From þe time þat þou was born" (l. 60). The other manuscripts conform to the reading in the "Auchinleck MS."

[6] *De Anima*, II, I, 402a, 20-30; 412b; 413a; 414a, 15-20.

[7] St. Thomas, *Trinity and the Unicity of the Intellect*, translated by Sister Rose Emmanuella Brennan (St. Louis: Herder, 1946), p. 243.

[8] Aristotle, *op. cit.*, 414a, 15-20.

[9] *Ibid.* In speaking of the soul's presence in the body, Grosseteste says it is wholly present in an *animated* body. "Sicut autem Deus simul totus est ubique in universo, ita anima simul tota est ubique in corpore animato." "De Intelligentiis," Baur, *op. cit.*, p. 114.

would seem from the context, then, that the dreamer, whether he realized it or not as the poet does not speculate or rationalize, had recourse to the plurality of forms, as Grosseteste had. The knight, then, derived from one form, the vegetable soul, his existence as a living thing; from another form, the sensitive soul, his existence as an animal; and from yet another form, his rational soul, his existence as a knight. The knight in that case was not absolutely one being, not one animal, not one man. According to the philosophy of Saint Thomas Aquinas, that would, of course, be absurd. It is from the same principle that one is a man, an animal, and a living thing.[10]

Saint Thomas defines the human soul as the first principle of the phenomena and activities of life, immanent in all living beings, whose noblest acts are self-movement and knowledge. The soul, therefore, cannot be corporeal, for something corporeal, though it can be a principle of life, as the eye or the heart, cannot be the *first* principle, the ultimate, immanent basis of life. Saint Thomas subscribes to the Aristotelian definition of the soul as the basic act *(actus)* of a physical organism capable of life.[11] He speaks, then, for a single soul in the individual man, a spiritual soul. This soul, which is numerically one, is the principle of intellectual, sensory, and vegetative life in the individual man; it is the source of the intellectual and the perceptual faculties, of the physical life of man.[12]

If the intellectual soul is not the form of the body, the question arises as to how this knight in the poem was able to think. This problem did not exist for the dreamer, as his illustration of this abstract principle by imagery reveals. His analogy of the horse and rider explains his position regarding the relationship that exists between the soul and the body.

---

[10] St. Thomas Aquinas. *Summa Contra Gentiles*, II, LVII; *Summa Theologica*, I^a, LXXVI, iii.

[11] *Summa Theologica*, I^a, LXXV, i.

[12] *Ibid.*, LXXVI, iii.

> Wedir I ede up or doun,
> þat I ne bar þe on my bac,
> Als þin as fro toun to toun, *Laud* (ll. 137-139)

> Or whare zede ich vp and doun,
> Day y no bare þe at mi bac,
> And was þine hors fram toun to toun "Auch." (ll. 281-283)

In these lines spoken by the Body, the Body identifies itself with the horse and the Soul with the rider. It may be assumed, it seems, that when one speaks of the rider's ability to understand, the reference is not to the man-and-horse together but to the man alone, though it is true that he is called the rider because he is suited to the task of controlling the horse. The understanding is attributed to the rider alone; and in like manner *to understand* will not be the act of the knight, but of the intellect alone which makes use of the body of the knight. Hence for the poet the soul is the man as Plato,[13] Saint Augustine,[14] and Hugh of St. Victor[15] understood it to be.

---

[13] Plato holds that man is not constituted of body and soul, but of a soul using or possessing a body. For him the whole personality can be found in the soul; so the separated soul can truly be man. Man is not a thing composed of body and soul but the soul itself "using a body is a man." I *Alcibiades*, 130 B-D, translated by W. R. Lamb. Loeb Library. (New York: G. Putnam's Sons, 1927), VIII, 199-201.

[14] For St. Augustine as for Plotinus, man is a very strange creature, half spirit and half animal. The Augustinian definition of the soul is identical with his definition of man. St. Augustine says that neither the soul taken separately nor the body taken separately is the man, but a soul which uses the body. But when asked to define the soul itself, he answers that it is a rational substance apt to rule the body. *De Quantitate Animæ*, XIII, 22; *PL*, XXXII, 1048. Man is really a soul using a body and in many respects he would be better off if the soul were not joined to a corruptible body. Bernard J. Cooke, S.J. ["The Mutability-Immutability Principle in St. Augustine's Metaphysics," *Modern Schoolman*, XIII (1946), footnote 57, 184] observes that the "unity of man is closer in St. Augustine than in his Platonic predecessors. Not that St. Augustine gives any rational grounds for a true union of body and soul but he seems to realize that man as Plato and Plotinus conceived him was out of place in the world of Christian revelation." See also A. Pegis, "In Defence of St. Augustine," *The New Scholasticism*, XVIII (1944), 117-118. Cooke, *loc. cit.*, further remarks that "this

The Soul reiterates the words of the Body and concurs that it has been borne about:

> ...Is no doute;
> Abouten, bodi, þou me bar;
> þou mostist nede, I was wiþoute
> Hand and fot, I was wel war. (ll. 161-164)

There is an intimation here, it seems, that their constant association was not voluntary, at least on the part of the Soul. Necessity required the Soul to be borne about, because it had no hands and feet. It is clear, then, that the soul needed the body to move. *Hand and foot* are the instruments of locomotion, and are reminiscent of Plato who regards the body as a vehicle and the members as instruments.[16] The implication is, too, that the soul moves essentially. Since there is no more intimate contact between the body and the soul than there is between the

---

realization is one that appears to have grown upon St. Augustine, for it is noted in his writings that there was a progressively greater stress on the union of the body and soul and a tendency away from the view that the body of its nature hinders the soul." Cooke calls attention to contrast, for example, a passage like that in the *Solil*. I, XIV, 24; *PL*, XXXII, 882, where Reason speaks of the soul as "in hac cavea inclusa," with St. Augustine's letter to Jerome: "Sed in alia superiore vita peccare animas et inde præcipitari in carceres carneos, non credo, non acquiesco, non consentio." Epistle CLXVI, clx, 27; *PL*, XXXIII, 732. See also *De Civ. Dei*, X, XXIX; *PL*, XLI, 308; and XIV, XI, 418.

[15] Hugh of St. Victor does not say that the soul is the form of the body, nor does he describe body and soul as complete separated substances, but his treatment is decidedly in the Platonist-Augustinian spirit. He regards the soul alone as the man. Hugh compares the body to an appendage which does not enter into the essential definition of a human person. *De Sacr.*, 2, I, II; *PL*, CLXXVI, 407D.

[16] Compare *Timæus* II, 69, translated by R. G. Bury. Loeb Library. (New York: G. Putnam's Sons, 1929), VII, 177: "And He [God] Himself acts as the Constructor of things divine, but the structure of mortal things He commanded to His own engendered sons to execute. And they, imitating Him, on receiving the immortal principle of the soul, framed around it a mortal body, and gave it all the body to be its vehicle, and housed therein besides another form of soul, even the mortal form, which has within it passions both fearful and unavoidable...."

horse and the rider, the soul is joined to the body not as form to matter but as mover to something movable or as a motor to what is moved. The relation between the body and the soul becomes, then, one of virtual contact[17] or, according to another term, of unity of action. But as Saint Thomas has pointed out, the difficulty with such a solution is that man is not a real unity; because things united by contact are not one simply.[18] Unity of action is not unity of existence. To be agent is not the same as *to be;* and therefore unity in action is not the same as is unity in being.[19] In the light of the horse-and-rider relation it appears as though the soul is joined to the body as one complete being to another. It cannot be otherwise inasmuch as the animating functions of the soul are not included in the poet's definition of the very essence of the soul, and union of soul and body remain an accident without any metaphysical necessity.

In keeping with the horse-and-rider relation of the body

---

[17] St. Thomas Aquinas, *Summa Contra Gentiles*, II, LVI and LVII.

[18] *Ibid.*, LVI: "Quæ autem uniuntur secundum talem contactum, non sunt unum simpliciter;...sic enim dicitur esse unum quomodo et ens; esse autem agens non significat esse simpliciter; unde nec esse unum in agendo est esse unum simpliciter."

[19] *Ibid.* Compare with Plotinus who in the *First Ennead* says: "From this relation, the Soul using the body as an instrument, it does not follow that the Soul must share in the body's experiences: a man does not himself feel all the experiences of the tools with which he is working.... Body may communicate qualities or conditions to another body; but — body to Soul?...As long as we have agent and instrument, there are always two distinct entities; if the Soul uses the body, it is separate from it... — or there might be part of the Soul detached and another part in contact, the disjoined part being agent and user, the conjoined part ranking with the instrument or thing used....It will be the task of philosophy to direct this lower Soul towards the higher, the agent, and except in so far as the conjunction is absolutely necessary, to sever the agent from the instrument, the body, so that it need not forever have its Act upon or through this inferior. Now the Couplement (of soul and body) subsists by virtue of the Soul's presence." *Plotinus: The Ethical Treatises Being the Treatise of the First Ennead*, translated from the Greek by Stephen MacKenna (London: The Medici Society, Limited, 1917), I, 1.3.

and soul, the Soul places the seat of the soul in the breast:[20] "Me þat þou bar in þi brest" (l. 192). Implied in this image is also the metaphor of the body as a house, a common figure in literature.[21] Saint Thomas declares that to conceive of the soul as present in the heart in its essence is to think of it as occupying the body spatially, as if it were only the motor and not the *form* of the body. He observes that according to such a conception the soul would be in the body as a sailor is in the ship, as Plato and Saint Albert the Great have declared;[22] or in the words of the Soul and Body in the poem, the soul is in the body as a rider is on his horse. Saint Thomas further affirms that to think of the soul as occupying a determinate part of the body in its essence is to conceive of its simplicity and indivisibility after the manner of a point, and thus to think of it also as something indivisible inhabiting an indivisible place.[23]

---

[20] It may be assumed that the poet had some indirect knowledge of the teaching of the *Timæus* as expounded by Chalcidius. See *Platonis Timæus interprete Chalcidio cum ejusdem commentario*, edited by J. Wrobel (Leipzig: B. G. Teubner, 1876), 220, p. 255: "Sicut aranea in medietate cassis omnia filorum tenet pedibus ex ordia, ut cum quid ex bestialis plagas incurrerit ex quacumque parte, de proximo sentiat, sic animæ principale, positum in media sede cordis, sensuum ex ordia retinere, ut, cum quid nuntiabunt de proximo recognoscat." See also the explanation of the position of Chalcidius in Etienne Gilson's *Philosophy of St. Bonaventure*, translated by Dom Illtyd Trethowan (New York: Sheed and Ward, 1937), p. 334: "According to this [Chalcidius in his commentary on the *Timæus*] the soul resides in its essence in a determinate part of the body, but it is capable of exercising its influence from there upon the whole body just as a spider feels from the center of its web the smallest impact of an insect at one of its extremities. The seat of the soul is in the heart, an organ placed in the middle of the body, whence sensation and movement derive, injury to which involves the separation of the body and the soul."

[21] For a brief treatment see A. Taylor, "A Metaphor of the Human Body in Literature and Tradition," *Corona. Studies in Celebration of the 80th Birthday of Samuel Singer* (Durham: Duke University Press, 1941), pp. 1 ff.

[22] *Supra*, p. 34, note 79.

[23] St. Thomas Aquinas, I, *Sent.*, d. 8, V, iii, VII, 123: "Respondeo dicendum, quod quidam posuerunt animam dupliciter posse considerari: aut secundum suam essentiam, aut secundum quod est quoddam totum potentiale. Si primo modo, sic dicebant, ipsam non esse in toto corpore, sed in aliqua parte ejus, scilicet corde, et per cor vivificare totum corpus

In the Soul's line of thinking, then, not every part of the body has existence through the soul as its form, since it is spatially located; in consequence the soul cannot feel with equal readiness an injury in any part of the body, as Chalcidius in his commentary on the *Timæus* would have it.[24]

The powers of the soul, it may be observed with Saint Thomas, are in the various organs of the body according to the various dispositions. Once it is held that the soul is joined to the body as its form and therefore completely to each part, it may be said, as Saint Augustine and Saint Thomas have said when they considered the operations of the soul, that the soul operates through the heart. But this refers to the operation of the soul in the body; it does not refer to the union of the soul and body.[25]

From this horse-and-rider-relationship can result only the unity of motion, not the unity of being; it will follow, therefore, that the body does not have *being* from the soul; and since life is a kind of being, it will follow also that the body does not have life from the soul, as Saint Thomas

---

per spiritus vitales procedentes a corde. Si secundo modo, sic anima consideratur ut quædam potentia integrata ex omnibus particularibus potentiis, et sic tota anima est in toto corpore, et non tota in qualibet parte corporis.... Hujus autem positionis causa, fuit duplex falso imaginatio: una est, quia imaginati sunt animam esse in corpore sicut in loco, ac si tantum esset motor, et non forma, sicut est nauti in navi; alia est, quia imaginati sunt simplicitatem animæ esse ad modum puncti, ut sit aliquid indivisibile habens situm indivisibilem. Ex utrumque horum stultum est."

[24] St. Augustine (*De Trinitate*, VI, 6, 8; *PL*, XLII, 929) and St. Bonaventure (I *Sent.*, d. 8, p. 2, a. i, III) hold with St. Thomas that the soul is in the body *tota in qualibet parte*. Hugh of St. Victor and the whole Victorine School repeat the Plotinian and Augustinian formula of the whole soul present in the whole body and in every part of it. *Summa Sententiarum*, I, *PL*, CLXXVI, 49D-50A.

[25] St. Thomas, in I *Sent.*, d. 8, V, iii, VII, 124, uses the term *motor* in connection with the activities carried on by the soul in the body in accordance with the various organs and their degree of complexity. Its use does not refer to the relation of the soul and the body. "Unde si consideratur anima prout est forma et essentia, est in qualibet parte corporis tota; si autem prout est motor secundum potentias suas, sic est tota in toto, et in diversis partibus secundum diversas potentias."

clearly indicates.²⁶ The unity of man requires that there be a unique principle of existence in the composite, and as it is the soul which is the principle of man's existence, it must be through the soul that man exists. But, if the dreamer is in line with Plato and his followers, and thus far there is every indication that he is, this difficulty does not exist for him, for he places the whole nature of man in the soul by presenting man as a soul possessing a body. For Plato self-motion is the very idea and essence of the soul. The body which is moved from without is soulless; but that which is moved from within has a soul, for such is the nature of the soul.²⁷

In *The Debate* the Body's own words testify to the principle of plurality of forms, as has been mentioned earlier in this chapter:

> I scholde have ben dumb as a schep,
> Or as an ouwe or as a swyn (ll. 153-154)

The Body remarks that as long as it was a companion of the Soul, locomotion, sight, hearing, and nutrition functioned. This would indicate that the soul as the enlightening or the rational principle possessed also other powers. It may be, therefore, that the dreamer identifies the powers of the soul with its very essence.²⁸

---

²⁶ *Summa Contra Gentiles*, II, LVII. "Adhuc, Mobile non habet esse per suum motorem, sed solum motum: Si igitur anima uniatur corpori solummodo, ut motor, corpus movebitur quidem ab anima, sed non habebit esse per eam. Vivere autem est quoddam esse viventis. Non igitur corpus vivet per animam."

²⁷ *Phædrus*, 287, I, 471.

²⁸ Most writers of the twelfth century followed St. Augustine and did not distinguish between the soul and its operations. For them the soul acts directly by its essence. They speak of a succession of acts, not of a distinction of powers which act. St. Augustine, *De Trinitate*, IX, 4, 5; *PL*, XLII, 963-964: "Admonemur, si utcunque videre possumus hæc in animo existere...substantialiter...non tanquam in subjecto, ut color, ...in corpore...quia etsi relative dicuntur ad invicem,...singula tamen substantialiter sunt in substantia sua." Among those who followed Augustine were Gregory the Great, Isidore of Seville, Alcuin, Rhaban Maur, William of St. Thierry, William of Auvergne. See H. Ostler,

> For al þe wile þou were mi fere
> I hadde al þat me was ned,
> I miȝte speke, se and here,
> I ede and rod and drank and et. (ll. 145-148)

These powers may be grouped into what Scholastics called the three main grades of life which included all others — the intellectual, sensitive, and vegetative. Today, *speech* is restricted to the rational life, because it is the outward expression of man's higher life. In early medieval times it was, according to the *New English Dictionary*,[29] on occasion, loosely included among the outward or bodily and the inward or ghostly senses.[30] Sight, hearing, and locomotion are also sensitive functions, but eating and drinking are nutritive acts. These acts, as indicated above, were performed only while the Body and the Soul were companions; i.e., the two are distinct and disparate substances in the sense that Plato[31] and Saint Augustine[32] held that during sensation, for example, the soul was active and the body passive.

For Plato sensation is a movement of the soul itself, which senses; and the soul being thus moved is moved by the body to sensation. When he defines sense, he says that

---

Die Psychologie des Hugo von St. Viktor (Muenster: i. W. Aschendorf, 1906), *BGPM*, VI, I, 90-91. Hugh of St. Victor quotes St. Augustine on this problem of the soul and its operations, but does not follow him in the prevalent opinion. Hugh admits a distinction between the soul and its faculties. The soul acts through its faculties, but the distinction is reduced to a minimum. The faculties are affections or accidents. Faculties are not the soul; they are in the soul. *De Sacr.*, I, III, 25; *PL*, CLXXVI, 227B.

[29] IX, I, 560.

[30] See *Ancren Riwle*, edited with translation by James Morton (London: Camden Society, 1853), p. 65, where the author in discussing the unrestrained use of the tongue classes speaking and tasting with sight and hearing: "Spellunge & smecchunge beoþ ine muþe boþe, ase sihþe is iþen eien...." Also, page 74, "...vor bridel nis nout one iþe horses muþe; auh sit sum up o þen eien & sum oþen earen."

[31] *Laws*, translated into English by R. G. Bury. Loeb Library. (New York: G. Putnam's Sons, 1926), II, Bk. 10, 896, 337-341.

[32] *Confessions*, VII, 17; *PL*, XXXII, 745.

it is a movement through the soul.³³ But to sense is logically not to move but to be moved. The sense itself is in passive potency of the organ affected by the external sensible object. During an act of sensation the sensitive soul is not active because, as Saint Thomas³⁴ has pointed out, it has no operation other than to inform the body which is being affected through the senses. Sensation requires the body as subject. To allow any activity to the soul in sensation would be equivalent to making an animal soul self-subsistent.³⁵

The Body admits that since the departure of the Soul its character has been changed.

> Loþli chaunged is my chere
>   Sin þe tyme þat þou me let;
> Def and dumb I ligge on bere,
>   þat I ne may sterin hand ne fet. (ll. 149-152)

The Body is loathsome and lies deaf and dumb on the bier, unable to move hand and foot. The Soul's testimony bears out this point:

> þine eiȝene are blinde and connen nouȝt kenne,
>   þi mouth is dumb, þin ere is def;
> And nou so loþli þou list grenne,
>   Fro þe comeþ a wikke wef. (ll. 117-120)

---

³³ See St. Thomas, *Summa Theologica*, Iª, LXXV, iii, where he remarks that Plato made of sensation an incorporeal function. St. Augustine regards the soul as the agent of sensation: "sentire non est corporis, sed animæ per corpus...." *De Genesi ad Litteram*, III, 5, 7; *PL*, XXXIV, 282. Vernon Bourke [*Augustine's Quest of Wisdom* (Milwaukee: The Bruce Publishing Company, 1945), pp. 111-112] refers to St. Augustine's theory of sensation as a partial interaction theory. He declares that "Augustine did not so radically separate body and soul that neither could act upon the other.... We have in Augustine a one-way, or unilateral, interactionism. For him the soul can, and does, act upon the body which is its inferior; but the body cannot act, or react, upon the soul." Compare: "Has operationes passionibus corporis puto animam exhibere cum sentit, non easdem passiones recipere." *De Musica*, VI, 5, 10; *PL*, XXXII, 1169. See also Othmar Knappke, C.PP.S., *The Scholastic Theory of Species Sensibiles*, Ph.D. Dissertation of The Catholic University of America (Washington: The Catholic University of America Press, 1915).

³⁴ *Contra Gentiles*, II, LVII.

³⁵ *Ibid.*, II, LXXXII; *Summa Theologica*, Iª, LXXV, iii.

It agrees that since the departure of the soul the body's parts are no longer human — the eyes are blind, the ears deaf, the mouth dumb — because they do not retain proper operations which are specifically human. It takes for granted that with the departure of the rational principle all life departs.

The Body further declares but for the direction that the Soul had given it, it would have been dumb as a sheep or a ewe or a swine that ate, drank, and lay down and slept, and would have suffered no worse fate than the lower creatures, for with their bodies die also their souls; nor would it have passed to the place of torment.

> I scholde have ben dumb as a schep,
>   Or as an ouwe or as a swyn
> Þat et and drank and lai and slep,
>   Slayn, and passid al his pin;
> Nevere of catel nome kep,
>   Ne wyste wat was water ne wyn,
> Ne leyn in helle þat is so dep,
>   Ne were þe wit þat al was þin. (ll. 153-160)

It is assumed by the Body that the non-rational life — the vegetative and the sensitive life — with its appetites and passions belongs to man only because the rational soul dwells in a material body.[36] Here the Body admits it is the rational power of the soul that elevates man above the level of the brute, and it makes reason and intelligence two separate faculties of intellectual activity. This can be deduced from the lines — "Ne wyste wat was water ne wyn" (l. 158) — which implies *reason* and — "Ne were þe wit

---

[36] The Body's bewailing that it was fated to be a human being appears also in the *Noctis sub Silencio Tempore Brumali* and in the "Old English Address of the Lost Soul to Its Body." But in these pieces the lines are spoken by the soul, not the body. This is the only Old English theme that does not appear in the *Worcester Fragments*, the transitional piece between the address and the debate. The Old French *Un Samedi par Nuit* agrees on this point with *The Debate*.

þat al was þin," (l. 160) — which implies *intelligence*. Two other lines bear out this point:

> For God þe schop aftir his schaft,
> And gaf þe boþe *wyt* and *skil;* (ll. 49-50)

God has created the soul and given it reason and intelligence.

In Boethius, who was a powerful influence in the Middle Ages, there is a sharp distinction of object and mode between reason and intelligence. Reason finds its object on a lower plain in sensible things, known in their universal aspect by discursive reasoning.[37] In the highest point of the mind *(acies mentis)* intelligence attains its primary object — the vision of God. It soars above created things to be lost in the contemplation of the pure and simple form of divinity.[38] Intelligence bears the stamp of divine origin in it, and indeed, it is called the divine faculty.[39] Hugh of St. Victor will agree with Saint Thomas that reason and intelligence are not two separate faculties but two aspects of intellectual activity. For Saint Thomas understanding *(intellectus)* deals with first principles and reason concerns itself with conclusions. The variety of meanings in Middle English often renders it difficult to assign particular examples to a definite sense. But up to the thirteenth century the word *skill* was another term for reason as a faculty of the mind, or the power of discrimination. But from the thirteenth to the fourteenth century it im-

---

[37] *Consolations of Philosophy*, V, Prose 4, edited with English translation by H. F. Stewart and E. K. Rand. Loeb Library. (Cambridge: Harvard University Press, 1936). On the semantics of *ratio-intelligentia* in Boethius, Augustine, Gundisalvi, etc., see G. Ed. Demers, "Les divers sens du mot Ratio au Moyen Age," in *Etudes d'Histoire Litteraire et Doctrinale du XIIIe Siècle*, première série (Ottawa: Insti. d'Etudes Medievales, 1932), 105-139.

[38] Boethius, *op. cit.*, V, 4, remarks: "Intelligentiæ vero celsior oculus exsistit; supergressa namque universitatis ambitum ipsam illam simplicem formam pura mentis acie contuetur."

[39] *Ibid.*, V, prose 4, 100.

plied discrimination or discretion in relation to special circumstances, or a sense of what is right and wrong.[40]

But for the Body to say, as it has said above, that it would have been dumb as a sheep had it not been for the Soul, which has been defined as the principle of understanding, not of animation, would presuppose that its sensitive life is not a part of the rational life; hence the body has a form of its own, as has been stated previously. Since the sensitive soul is, then, the form of the body, the intellect is, thereby, freed from any condition of materiality. According to Saint Thomas this theory again violates the unity of man; a particular man understands because the intellectual principle is his form.[41] The intellectual soul must become the form of the body in one act of existence from which will be derived all the operations of life from the lowest to the highest.[42] The body is not necessary to the intellectual soul by reason of the intellectual operation considered as such; but because of the sensitive power which requires an organ of equable temperament, the intellectual soul needs to be united to such a body. But the sensitive power the dreamer places in the intellectual soul —

> For al þe wile þou were mi fere
> I miȝte speke, se and here, (ll. 145 and 147)

which to him is not the animating principle, as has been pointed out before.

The Body in its turn asserts that all knowledge of right and wrong comes from the Soul and places the responsibility for its conduct in the Soul.

> Ȝwat wist I wat was wrong or riht,
> Wat to take or ȝwat to schone,
> Bote þat þou pottest in mi siȝht
> þat al þe wisdom scholdest cone? (ll. 217-220)

---

[40] *NED*, IX, I, 138.
[41] *Contra Gentiles*, II, LVIII.
[42] *Summa Theologica*, Iᵃ, LXXVI, i, *Resp.*

It declares that it could not distinguish between right and wrong, nor make a choice, but that the soul possessed these powers. If the body is everywhere penetrated by the soul; if flesh, muscles, nerves, derive from the soul their qualification of human, then it can be easily understood that not only man's physical life, but also his psychic life is closely bound up with the organism. Sensations and sense desires, which man possesses in common with other animals, have their seat in the organism, though the dreamer does not hold this. Since they are in the organism, they are in consequence extended and divisible. In case of abstract and universal concepts, scientific judgment and reasoning, the willing of good in general and the free choice of particular goods, the soul is still held to the organism, since a disease of the nerves is sufficient to prevent the use of reason and to diminish or destroy liberty. But the normal condition of the body is only an *external condition:* it is not responsible for the existence of thought or will in their very essence. Thought and will are superior to everything that is material, because the human concept has the power of extending its dominion over reality, in depriving it, by abstraction, of all that makes it merely corporeal.

But the Body continues:

> þou þat was so worþli wrouȝt,
> To seye I made þe my þral?
> Did I nevere on live nouȝt,
> I ne rafte ne I ne stal
> þat first of þe ne cam þe þouȝt;
> Aby it þat abyȝe schal! (ll. 211-216)

The Body flings the responsibility for sin at the feet of the Soul by reason of the fact that it has been created in the image and likeness of God and that all thought for the act, specifically plundering and stealing, has come from the Soul. It is through the spiritual soul, so the Body says, that man is made in the image and likeness of God. It is true, according to Saint Thomas, that every act of the will depends upon

an act of the intellect, since the will becomes active only
when the cognitive faculty presents an object to it. Knowledge by its guidance and direction and will by its command
unite in action to effect a common result. The will is the
motor power of the soul's activities (except the vegetative
faculty) and thus the will is the mover of reason and the
intellect.[43] But in every thought, in every action, man uses
his material body. No thought, then, can ever pass through
the mind for one brief moment but the body takes part in
it, inasmuch as its activity supplies the phantasm upon
which the intellect operates.

The dreamer also considers the origin of the soul. The
Soul declares that both body and soul have been born of
woman.

> Of o wymman born and bredde,
> Body, were we boþe two; (ll. 169-170)

Each soul is created, then, in its own individual body, not
before it. It is spiritual; the Body says that the soul has
been fashioned in the image and likeness of God:

> For God þe schop aftir his schaft,
> And gaf þe boþe wyt and skil; (ll. 49-50)

The likeness is in the image; an image is like its archetype.
Just as a statue or a portrait, if it be a good one, is like
the person portrayed, so man (here the soul) is as the image
of God; he imitates, reproduces, is a replica of the attributes of God. It would seem here that the soul is created
by a special act on the part of God. It did not exist before
the body.[44]

The poet does not follow Plato in making the body the

---

[43] *Summa Theologica*, Iª IIae, IX, i ad iii.

[44] For Plato the human soul was framed before the body. "God, however, constructed the Soul to be older than Body and prior in birth and
excellence, since she was to be the mistress and rule and it the ruled."
Timæus, 35, p. 65.

prison-house of the soul. With Saint Augustine and Hugh of St. Victor he holds that the soul loves the body,[45] for the Soul remarks:

> I saw þe fair on fleysch and blod
> And al mi love on þe I kest; (ll. 185-186)

> ...Bodi, allas, allas,
> þat I þe lovede evere ȝete,
> For al mi love on þe I las. (ll. 250-252)

The exclamation *allas* on the part of the Soul and its repetition carries a note of regret at having loved the Body; for the love lavished on the Body is lost.

And again

> Softe þe for love I ledde,
> Ne dorst I nevere do þe wo;
> To lese þe so sore I dredde, (ll. 173-175)

There is the recognition in these lines that the body and the soul were intended by nature to be joined to each other and that the Soul dreaded the loss of the Body. The soul has a natural inclination and appetite to perfect a corporeal substance, while the body has an appetite to receive the soul. But the Soul's motive for this careful and solicitous direction is that it feared loss of the present body would not guarantee another. Saint Augustine says that the soul naturally desires to be joined to the body, and by this he means that the "soul is created with such a nature as to desire this, in the same way as it is natural to us to desire to live."[46] But when the motives for the desire are considered, it is found that for Saint Augustine the soul enters the body as a messenger of light from divine ideas. The

---

[45] See *De Spiritu et Anima*, *PL*, XL, 789: "Sociata namque illi, licet ejus societate prægravetur, ineffabili tamen conditione diligit illud; amat carcerem suam."

[46] *De Genesi ad Litt.*, VII, 27, 38; *PL*, XXXIV, 369.

soul is nearer to the divine ideas than is the body; it is, therefore, more perfect than the body, and this priority of the soul is as it ought to be. Saint Thomas, on the other hand, holds firmly to the principle that the soul is joined to matter for its own good; the soul *needs* the body and it is incapable of doing its work as an intellectual substance unless it is joined to it. It is not the good of the body, but that of the soul which this union has in view.[47] In the poem, as the above lines reveal, the Soul is aware that if it loses the present body it will not receive another. But if the relationship between the body and soul is the rider-horse or motor-mobile relation, an accidental relationship, there should be no grief on the part of the soul to leave the body, for there is no difficulty in "withdrawal, since the relation of the body to the soul is like that of 'Brother Ass to his rider.' "[48]

In the study of the horse-and-rider analogy in this chapter, attention has been given to an analysis of the second reference, the psychological reference. Accordingly, in the poem there are two separate entities in man, the body and the soul. The soul is in the body as a pilot in the ship; consequently, there is lacking a unity of being. Both the speeches of the Body and of the Soul, either implicitly or expressly, bear testimony to this accidental relationship between the soul and the body. Logically, if the body and the soul are not one in *esse* they cannot be one in operation. There appears, however, a reluctance on the part of the

---

[47] *Summa Theologica*, Iᵃ, LXXXIV, iv. See also *Q. Disp. de Animæ*, viii ad xv: "Anima humana unitur corpori propter intelligere, quod est propria et principalis ejus operatio; et ideo requirit quod corpus unitum animæ rationali sit optime dispositum ad serviendum animæ in his quæ sunt necessaria ad intelligendum." Also *ibid.*, i ad vii: "Anima unitur corpori et propter bonum quod est perfectio substantialis, ut scilicet compleatur species humana; et propter bonum quod est perfectio accidentalis, ut scilicet perficiatur in cognitione intellectiva, quam anima ex sensibus acquirit; hic enim modus intelligendi est naturalis homini."

[48] Robert Brennan, O.P., *The History of Psychology* (New York: The Macmillan Company, 1946), p. 59.

soul to leave the body. This is not possible in an accidental relation. It may be that the poet was striving to effect an essential relationship. But, in his use of the horse-and-rider image in the poem, the poet was concerned primarily with its moral rather than with its psychological reference. His interest lay in moral instruction, not in philosophical theory.

As we turn to chapter III we shall consider the third reference — the ethical reference — of the horse-and-rider relation to see how man is ordered and what part the soul and the body play in sin.

CHAPTER III

THE ETHICAL MEANING OF THE ANALOGY

Although not essentially involved in the image of the horse and rider as such, the material in this chapter is relevant to the understanding of the functioning of that image or theme in *The Debate between the Body and the Soul*.

The rational life of our nature, *The Debate between the Body and the Soul* reveals, bears the imprint of the divine nature, for God has created the soul in His image and likeness (ll. 49-50). The non-rational life, the vegetative and the sensitive life with its appetites and passions, belongs to man only because the rational soul dwells in a material body (ll. 145-160). Moreover, it is through the non-rational life of man that such a union of the intelligible and sensible is possible. All these manifestations of man's non-rational life that exist in us are passions allotted to man to become instruments of the soul either for virtue or for vice, according to the use free will makes of them. If reason, the excellent part of our nature, holds its sway over the elements imparted from without, each of them is changed to form virtue. If, however, reason loses its hold, if it gives rein to these non-rational impulses, it, in turn, is dragged down and becomes gross; man's whole life, then, becomes brutish.

By means of the comparison of the body to a horse which the soul, as the rider, is unable to control the poet builds up his thesis in a dialogue of uncommon impressiveness and high dramatic power. He shows how the soul, once it has lost control of its irrational nature, is dragged by the unruly passions to the level of the brute just as the rider who has lost the reins of his horse is dragged wherever the irrational movements of the horse carry him. Therefore, there is no mistaking his thesis: the responsibility for the loss of the soul rests with the soul, for it has been assigned to direct the body (ll. 51-52).

After its tirade on the vanities of the worldly life as revealed in the *Ubi sunt?* motif, which has been referred to in chapter I, the Soul rebukes the body, charging it with leading the Soul into the occasions of sin: "Wiþ þi teþ þe bridel þou lauȝt" (l. 83). But the Body counters that wherever it went it bore the Soul on its back:

> Wedir I ede up or doun,
> þat I ne bar þe on my bac,
> Als þin as fro toun to toun,
> Alse þou me lete have rap and rac? (ll. 137-140)

The Body refers to itself as the beast of burden that bore the Soul, the holder of the reins, upon its back, adding also that it had accepted the blows and the beatings (hastiness and rashness) the Soul had administered. It is the horseman's business to subdue the horse and to use the bit when it disregards the rein. If the horseman keeps a lighter contact with the horse's mouth than is compatible with adequate control, the horse takes the bit between its teeth, thereby becoming unmanageable.[1]

The Body reminds the Soul that it was the ruler since the Body was left to its direction.

> In þi loking was I laft
> To wisse aftir þin oune wil. (ll. 51-52)

To wisse means to advise or direct according to the will of the Soul. If the Body took the bit into its teeth, the responsibility rests with the Soul who had control of the reins.[2]

---

[1] *NED*, I, 881.

[2] Compare Hoccleve, *Regement of Princes and Fourteen Minor Poems*, edited by F. J. Furnivall (London: *EETS ES*, 72, 1897), "The Epistle of Grace Dieu,"- p. xxvi: "Shamë hath he þat at the cheker pleith/ Whan þat a powne saith to the kyng 'chek mate';/ And shame it is, whan that the gost obeith/ Vnto thi flessh, þat schuld obeye algate/ Vnto thi goost" (ll. 113 ff.).

The Soul readily admits that the Body was the beast of burden

> ...Is no doute;
> Abouten, bodi, þou me bar;
> þou mostist nede, I was wiþoute
> Hand and fot,... (ll. 161-164)

and a necessary instrument for the Soul; yet there is an intimation here in the lines:

> þou mostist nede, I was wiþoute
> Hand and fot,... (ll. 163-164)

that their constant association was not voluntary, at least on the part of the Soul. In attempting to clear itself of responsibility by shifting it to the Body, the Soul declares that without the Body it would not have gone to places which were an occasion of sin.

> Bote as tou bere me aboute
> Ne miȝt I do þe leste char;
> þorfore most I nede loute,
> So doth þat non oþer dar. (ll. 165-168)

But while joined to the Body, the Soul was forced to bow and to do obeisance to the Body — "þorfore most I nede loute" (l. 167). The Soul dared not do otherwise. The contextual implications in the line, "Ne miȝt I do þe leste char," (l. 166), are that the Soul of its own accord could not move.

The implication in these last lines spoken by the Soul is, clearly, that the powers of the flesh were so violent, the pull of concupiscence was so strong that the Soul was forced to accede to the Body's wishes. It may be said that the dreamer is aware of the irregularity in the soul, the tendency to evil inherited by every man from Adam and this same inclination intensified and strengthened by our personal sins and vices which have taken hold of the soul. Created in original justice, as the phrase ran, the powers of the soul were at first in perfect harmony. Man's sensitive nature, that is, his passions, were in subjection to his will, and his will to reason, and his reason to God. But Adam fell and in his fall his entire being was disturbed. Since this fall, the body and its appetites are perpetual impediments to the higher activities of the soul. This perennial conflict between reason and passion, Saint Thomas Aquinas observes, comprises the major portion of the drama of man's existence;[3] and when the struggle is over, passion frequently emerges as victor. Man lusts, although he will not lust; this is due to the disproportion whereby the sensitive appetite of the body is hindered from perfect compliance with the command of reason. So Saint Paul says, "For I do not understand what I do, for it is not what I wish that I do, but what I hate, that I do...I see another law in my members, warring against the law of my mind and making me prisoner to the law of sin that is in my members."[4] The law of the mind is the law of reason; but the law of the members is the law of passion. When man follows the rule of reason he conducts himself as is befitting a man, but when he follows the dictates of passion, the beast in him makes him an animal. The rider must hold empire over the horse, but when the reverse takes place, the rational faculty ceases to dominate the sense appetites, and reason is dethroned.

In consonance with the horse-and-rider analogy is the metaphor of the master and the servant. The master like the rider has the power of control and of protection, while the servant like the horse exerts himself for the benefit of his master.

Above, the Soul has admitted that the body bore it about, that it lacked hands and feet. It is agreed that the will governs the faculty of our exterior motion as a servant. The master rules his servant by force which he has no power to contradict. In like manner, unless some external thing hinders, the faculty of our exterior motion never

---

[3] See *Summa Theologica*, Iª IIae, LXXXII, i ad iii, for a discussion of the rebellion of man's senses against reason.

[4] Romans vii: 23.

fails to obey. Man opens his mouth, moves his tongue, his hands, feet, and eyes, and all the members to which the power of this movement refers, without resistance, according to his desire and will. The horse, on the other hand, the horseman must manage by industry, binding, bridling, and goading. Likewise, one's senses and faculties of nourishing, growing, producing, one must manage with industry and art, because one cannot govern them with the same ease as exterior motion. When the master calls his servant, he comes; when the master tells him to stop, he stops; but the horseman cannot expect this obedience from a horse. The master bids his servant to turn to the right or left and he does it; but to make a horse turn, the horseman does not command, but simply makes the horse do as he wishes by using the bridle. Again, man does not give orders of abstinence to the palate or stomach, but he commands the hands to furnish meat and drink in a measure that reason requires. If the eyes are not to see, he covers them and by that means he brings them to the point where the will desires them. It would be folly, though, to command a horse not to grow fat, not to kick — to effect this one must stop his corn, or use physical restraint. One does not command him; one makes him do as one wishes.

The Body readily admits its duties as a servant:

> Set to serven þe to queme
> Boþe at even and at morn,
> Siþin I was þe bitauȝt to ȝeme,
> Fro þe time þat þou was born. (ll. 57-60)

If the Soul was assigned guardianship of the Body (ll. 51-52), since the Body was committed to the Soul at birth, as the last line above reveals, it naturally follows that the Body was to be the servant at all times, and the phrase — "Boþe at even and at morn" — conveys in thought the period from birth to death. In the span of one's whole lifetime the soul holds sway — passion is always subservient to reason. But the more the Body seeks the protection of the Soul, the more the Soul becomes implicated in its care; and the more the Soul becomes implicated in its care, the more the Soul stays to enjoy where it should have stayed to rule. The Soul acknowledges this enslavement:

> þou dist al þat þe werld þe bad,
> And þat þi fleys þe wolde crave;
> I þolede þe and dide as mad
> To be maister and I þi cnave. (ll. 205-208)

Yet it strives to mitigate its own responsibility by charging that the Body yielded to the seductions of two — the world and the devil — of the three ghostly adversaries —[5] the world, the flesh, and the devil, which will be explained later.

The Body reproaches the Soul inasmuch as in the light of its position as the ruling principle it should have been aware of the Body's folly.

> þou þat dedes couþest deme
> Scholdest habbe be war biforn
> Of mi folye,... (ll. 61-63)

The Body acknowledges by implication that it is a profitable servant when held in check, an indispensable one, whose strength must be preserved to place it at the service of the Soul. Inasmuch as the Soul could judge the worth of deeds, it carried the responsibility. In *Of mi folye* is implied that in a state of fallen nature the Body seeks the joys of the flesh, regardless of what is licit or illicit; it has a special tendency towards forbidden pleasures, and at times rebels against the higher faculties when they stand in the way.

The Soul admittedly grants its awareness of the Body's tendency to evil:

> To sinne and schame it was þi drauȝt,
> Til untid and til wikkedehed; (ll. 85-86)

but it constructs its case by attempting to show that though it opposed the Body — "Inouȝ I stod ageyn and fauȝt,"

---

[5] The debate is about the three foes but only two — the world and the devil — are mentioned. The Body represents the flesh. See Mätzner, *op. cit.*, p. 98.

(l. 87) — the latter failed to listen and persistently followed its own inclination or counsel: "Bot ai þou nome þin oune red" (l. 88). But the Soul modifies this statement by conceding to the Body that in its early years it had performed deeds under the eyes of friends, as the following passage reveals.

> For me þou woldest sumwat do
> Wȝile þou were ȝong a litil first,
> For frendes eyȝe þat þe stod to,
> þe wile þou were betin and birst;
> Oc wan þou were þriven and þro,
> And knewe hunger, cold and þirst,
> And ȝhwilk was eyse, rest and ro,
> Al þin oune wil þou dist. (ll. 177-184)

The meaning of *frendes eyȝe* is actually the awe and fear of friends.[6]

The Soul argues that the Body submitted to physical discipline while young; that it was beaten and bruised with cold and hunger;[7] but as it grew older and stronger and learned more and more of the ways of the world and of a life of leisure, its thoughts became occupied with the sins of the flesh and of the spirit.

The Soul hurls an imposing list of social transgressions — all the seven deadly sins — into the teeth of the Body.

> Gloterie and lecherie,
> Pride and wicke coveytise,
> Niþe and onde and envie
> To God of hevene and alle hise,
> And in unlust for to lye,
> Was ti wone in alle wise;
> That I schal nou ful dere abye,
> A, weyle! sore may me grise. (ll. 193-200)

---

[6] *Ibid.*, p. 96. Compare "Ne sulen he non eige sen us on," (l. 2550). *The Story of Genesis and Exodus*, edited by Richard Morris (London: EETS OS, 7, 1865), p. 73.

[7] Compare "Buten he weoren ibirsted: mid hungere & mid þurste" (ll. 371). Layamon, *Brut* or *Chronicle of Britain*, edited by Sir Frederic Madden (London: Society of Antiquaries, 1847), II, 371.

The Soul begins with gluttony and lechery, sins of the flesh;[8] then continues on with pride, covetousness, envy and anger, sins of the spirit. *Niþe* is a synonym for envy as is also *onde*. But *onde*[9] has also another meaning — that of wrath, *anger*. The seventh and last of the sins mentioned by the Soul is *sloth*, which the poet expresses in terms of "And in unlust for to lye," meaning *to lie in displeasure*. Specifically, the sins for which condemnation comes in *The Debate* are pride and gluttony. The Body's propensities for hunting, riding, and for fine clothes and rich foods are called to mind in the *Ubi Sunt?* passage (ll. 25-48). All these sins the Soul links with the Body, sorely affrighted, however, that it must atone for them.

The motif of the seven deadly sins was traditional in sermons of the Middle Ages.[10] The medieval preacher laid constant stress on the danger of the deadly sins to man's soul and attributed their origin to his three unholy adversaries — the devil, the world, and the flesh. The devil, the

---

[8] St. Thomas distinguishes between carnal and spiritual sins. Accordingly, those sins which consist in spiritual pleasures are called spiritual sins, while those which consist in carnal pleasures are called carnal sins; e.g., gluttony, which consists in the pleasures of the table, and lust, which consists in sexual pleasures. *Summa Theologica*, I^a II^{ae}, LXXII, ii. Gregory the Great says that of the seven deadly sins five are spiritual and two carnal. *Moralia*, XXXI, 45; *PL*, LXXVI, 621. As early as the fifth century Cassian, *De Cœnobiorum Institutis* Libri Duodecim, Bks. IV to XII; *PL*, XLIX, 202-473, categorically sets forth the eight chief vices, pride being regarded as the worst of sins. After the time of Benedict the deadly sins became an integral part of Christian teaching and formed one of the most common themes in medieval literature.

[9] *The Anglo-Saxon Dictionary.* Based on the Manuscript Collections of the late Joseph Bosworth, edited and enlarged by T. Northcote Toller (Oxford: Clarendon Press, 1832), p. 722.

[10] See Abbot Gasquet, *Parish Life in Medieval England* (London: Metheun, 1907), p. 214: A ruling of the Synod of Oxford (1281) ordered that "every priest having charge of a flock, do, four times in each year (that is, once each quarter), on one or more solemn feast days, either himself or by some one else, instruct people in the vulgar language, simply and without fantastical admixture of subtle distinctions, in the Articles of the Creed, the Ten Commandments, the Evangelical Precepts, the seven works of mercy, the seven deadly sins with their off-shoots, the seven principal virtues, and the Seven Sacraments."

preacher observed, tempts to pride, wrath, and envy; the world, to covetousness; and the flesh to gluttony and lechery.[11]

The Body makes no attempt to deny what the Soul has said. But mindful of the old pithy saying, "As the twig is bent the tree is inclined," it meets the Soul on equal grounds.

>   Oc haddist þou, þat Crist it ouþe,
>   Given me honger, þirst and cold,
>   And þou witest me þat no god couþe,
>   In bismere ȝwan I was so bold,
>   þat I hadde undernomen in ȝouþe
>   I havede holden ȝwan I was old,
>   þou let me reykin north and south
>   And haven al my wille on wold. (ll. 225-232)

The Body is convinced, as the first three lines indicate, that only a life disciplined by mortification in early youth, would that Christ had granted it, would have enabled it steadfastly to withstand temptation. The Body chides the Soul for pinning the blame on one that could do no good. It realizes that victory or defeat in some sudden and violent assault of passion may depend upon whether one has practiced self-disci-

---

[11] See *Middle English Sermons*, edited by Woodburn O. Ross (London: EETS OS, 209, 1940), pp. 31-32: "Firste, I sey þou muste [be] shryven and full repentante and do penaunce for þe vij dedely synnes; þat is to sey, pryde, wrathe, and envye, þe wiche þe dewell tempeste þe in day by daye.... The fourte is couetyze, where-in þe worlde temptes þe in at all tyme, for þou canste not hold þe a payed with þoȝ goodes þat God haþ sende þe.... The v, þe vj, and vij beþ slouthe, glotenye, and lecherye; in þe wiche þi flessh temptes þe euermore. Aȝeyn þe synne of couetyz take and doþ almus dede. Aȝeyns slouthe vse preyoure; aȝeyns gloteny, fastynge; and aȝeyns lecherye, chastite." See also p. 270: "First, than [fight] manly aȝens þe devell, þe world and þe flessh, and ouercome them — ȝe, the seven devels þat beþ chef vppon the vij dedely synnes, as Lucifere, Mammona, Asmodeus, and oþur." Earlier homilies speak of eight deadly sins. See "Sermon on Sunday in Lent," *Twelfth Century Homilies*, p. 43; "Sermon Concerning the Eight Vices and the Twelve Abuses of this Age," *Old English Homilies of the Twelfth Century*, edited by Richard Morris (London: EETS ES, 29-34, 1873), pp. 100-107.

pline in such minor things as food or sleep or little acts of self-indulgence in youth.[12] The Body's words give testimony that the dreamer was alive to the teachings of Saint Paul, who emphasized the necessity of mortifying the flesh and bringing it into subjection to escape sin and final reprobation. "But I chastise my body and bring it into subjection, lest perhaps after preaching to others I myself should be rejected."[13] If the Body had been chastised in youth; if it had been inured to suffer hunger, thirst, and cold, all mortifications of the flesh, it would have been schooled to truth and righteousness and would have preserved its strength to place it at the Soul's service when it had grown older. The Body frankly accuses the Soul of having fallen short of its obligation in allowing it to ply free rein. — "þou let me reykin north and south" (1. 231). The Body should have been taught to wrestle with everything that tended to take hold upon it until it had taught each thing its proper place; then in the hour of temptation the will would not have failed it. From the Body's words it may be concluded that the attitude and bearing towards small things will decide the issue in those great moral conflicts upon which the welfare or the ruin of the Soul depends.

The Soul owns that it was lax in its proper direction of the Body.

> I saw þe fair in fleysch and blod
>   And al mi love on þe I kest;
> þat þou þrive me þouȝte god,
>   And let þe haven ro and rest. (ll. 185-188)

It admits that love and solicitude of and its concern for the welfare, peace, and quiet of the Body, upon which the Soul

---

[12] Compare the lines in John Myrc's sermon for Septuagesima Sunday: "The þryd ys forto chastes þy body dyscretly.... For mannys flesche ys so wyld and lusty to synne, þat hyt wyll no way leue his lust and serue þe soule tyll hit be chastet wyth penance; so þat, by scharpenes of penaunce, þe lyking of synne schall be slayne yn þe flessche þat doth þe synne." *Festial*, edited by Theodor Erbe (London: EETS OS, 96, 1905), p. 67.

[13] I Corinthians ix: 27.

had cast its love, inclined it toward leniency. But to mitigate its own responsibility the Soul asserts that the Body took advantage of the moratorium in the conflict between the spirit and the flesh and grew unruly, forcing the Soul to yield to the dictates of the flesh; for the former found no remedy for fighting against the flesh.

> þat made þe so stirne of mod,
> And of werkes so unwrest;
> To fiʒte with þe ne was no bot (ll. 189-191)

It may readily be observed that the Body had little regard for the strength of the Soul, under whose constant but easy surveillance it had walked at all times, as the following lines indicate:

> Were was I bi wode or weyʒe,
> Sat or stod or dide ouʒt mys,
> þat I ne was ay under þin eyʒe?
> Wel þou wost þat soth it is. (ll. 133-136)

and

> Oc for I þe so eise fond, (l. 237)

In no uncertain terms the Body lays the charge of sinning at the feet of the Soul, characterizing it with the power of distinguishing between right and wrong and of choosing between good and evil.

> ʒwat wist I wat was wrong or riht,
> Wat to take or ʒwat to schone,
> Bote þat þou pottest in mi siʒht
> þat al þe wisdom scholdest cone? (ll. 217-220)

The Body knows that judgment is not a mere assertion of the intellect but that it looks to the action of the will, as Saint Thomas Aquinas has also remarked.[14] But reason that with wisdom rules the whole nature in ordinary affairs of life becomes clouded and obscured in moral action.

---

[14] *Summa Theologica*, Iª IIae, IX, i.

Saint Thomas says that when an attractive object confronts any one of the senses, that particular sense can immediately reach out for the object quite independently of the will's consent and even against the will's command. By that very fact the will is weakened. Concupiscence pulls one toward the tempting object even though he realizes that taking it involves sin. One may have reached out to seize it before the mind adverts to what one is doing. And even after the mind does take notice the incitement still persists, the tug is still felt. One is much less able to resist the allurement than if the senses are fully under control. Man is torn between the higher and a lower good.[15]

The Body's description of itself in terms of a weak and flexible rod under the surveillance of an easy Soul

> þat ay was wriþinde as a wond,
> þerfore couþe I nevere blinne. (ll. 239-240)

aptly illustrates the insecurity with which one walks the moral road in the company of a Soul with such "thin wit" (And þi wretche wit so þinne, l. 238), so dispossessed of reason. Under such guidance the Body could not cease sinning. This image fittingly prepares for the next stanza, where the blind lead the blind.

> To sinne þou wistist was my kinde,
> As mankinne it is al so,
> And to þe wretche world so minde,
> And to þe fend þat is ure fo.
> Þou scholdest er have late me binde
> Wan I misdede, and don me wo;
> Ac ȝwanne þe blinde lat þe blinde,
> In dike he fallen boþe two. (ll. 241-248)

The Body is convinced that as long as the Soul realized the weakness of the flesh and its predilection for the world and the devil, the Soul should not have allowed the Body to go blindly into sin. If the Body could have been brought into proper subjection to the Soul, the devil and the world

---

[15] *Ibid.* Iª IIᵃᵉ, IX, ii and iii; LXXXI, ii; LXXXII, iii.

would have been powerless against the flesh. The Body would impress upon the Soul that the bodily senses are blind — blind towards the fulfillment of the divine will; blind to the benefits conferred upon the Soul; blind even to its salvation. Therefore, it will be woeful for the Soul that will follow such a leader. Reason blinded by passion must inevitably lead to destruction, for if the blind lead the blind both fall into the pit.[16]

It must not be supposed, however, that the Soul lost sight of the spiritual assistance that is needed in carrying on its work toward salvation. Further grievances against the Body are its neglect of the duties of a Christian.

> I bad þe þenke on soulenedes,
>   Matines, masse, and evesong;
> Thou mostist first don oþere dedes,
>   þou seidist al was idel gong. (ll. 97-100)

Man can of his own accord fall into sin; but sin in its nature is final and irrevocable, for man is completely unable by himself even to remove the smallest sin. To advance towards merit he needs divine assistance, which is borne to him by the ministry of the angels. At this point the Soul does not recommend confession of sin as it does later, but it urges attention to the liturgical prayers — matins and vespers — and the liturgical act, Mass, all of which, in spite of the protests of the flesh, will strengthen in the spirit that divine energy which will enable it to endue the Body with its strength.[17] But the Soul complains that the Body dis-

---

[16] Matthew xv: 14; Luke xvi: 39.

[17] The above grievances are the main theme of "A Thirteenth Century Fragment," *MS Coll. Trinity B. 14, 39*, in Thomas Wright, *The Latin Poems Commonly attributed to Walter Mapes*, Appendix 322. This fragment of twenty-four lines describes how, after the man has been put into the grave, the soul addresses the body, complaining that for the neglect of its Christian duties the body must dwell in a coffin to be chewed by worms. In these grievances may be heard also the voice of the clergy who wanted to inculcate in the minds of their parishioners that only diligent observance of duties to the Church and its representatives would avert the doom that otherwise awaited them.

missed these suggestions lightly by declaring them idle matters — "þou seidist al was idel gong (l. 100) — and diverted its attentions to what seemed more important to the Body, that is, to sports and games (ll. 101-104).

These grievances about the neglect of Christian duties are not especially characteristic of *The Debate between the Body and the Soul*, for they are really part and parcel of all literary pieces dealing directly with the Body and Soul theme.[18]

But the Soul introduces another element — the unholy trinity comprising the three great powers of the devil, the world, and the flesh; these ghostly adversaries, who are the constant foes of the Christian man, made their appearance in vernacular religious writings in the twelfth century.[19] These three foes constitute an important element in the structure of the Soul's argument, since the Body has joined conspiracy with the devil and the world against the Soul.

>Þe fend of helle þat haveþ envie
>   To mankinne, and evere haþ had,
>Was in *us* as is a spie
>   To do sum god ȝwan I þe bad.
>The werld he toc to cumpaynie,
>   Þat mani a soule haved forrad;
>Þey þre wisten þi folye,
>   And maden, wretche, þe al mad. (ll. 257-264)

It is possible that the Soul mentions the fiend first because he is the leader, or the most powerful, of these ghostly

---

[18] This list of grievances appears also in "Old English Address," *Worcester Fragments, Un Samedi par Nuit*, and *Noctis sub Silencio Tempore Brumali*.

[19] See "Induite Uos Armatura Dei," *Old English Homilies*, 29, p. 240: "These three foes are — the devil and his host, the second is the earth, the third is very near the Christian man, that is, his own flesh." Also in *Old English Homilies*, 34, p. 204; and *Middle English Sermons*, pp. 111, 270. The adversaries are treated also in the "Sayings of St. Bernard: Man's Three Foes" in *Minor Poems of the Vernon Manuscript*, edited by F. J. Furnivall (London: EETS OS, 117, 1901), pp. 511-522; "The Castel of Love" by Bishop Robert Grosseteste in *Minor Poems of the Vernon Manuscript*, Part I, edited by Carl Horstman (London: EETS OS, 98, 1892), 355-394.

enemies. This explains his intervention in the life of man by reference to his envy[20] which prompts him to edge his way into man's soul to hinder his progress. With the world he joined in compact and then these two leagued themselves with the flesh, thereby establishing the infernal trio that is ever at war with man from the time that he leaves the baptismal font, where divine life is planted in the soul, until his death. The contextual reference is to three enemies — "þey þre wisten þi folye" (l. 263) — who had knowledge of the weakness of the flesh. In reality only two enemies are left to be cognizant of it — the wiles of the devil and the incursions of the world.[21]

The Soul constructs its argument by hurling a threefold accusation against the Body.

> ʒwan I bad þe reste take,
>   Forsake sinne ay and oo,
> Do penaunce, faste and wake,
>   þe fend seide, 'þou schalt nouʒt so,
> þus sone al þi blisse forsake,
>   To liven ay in pine and wo! *Laud* (ll. 265-270)

The "Auchinleck" text is more definite than the *Laud* in this stanza; the former discloses that the Soul had bidden the Body to shrive itself.

> When y bad þe schrift take,
>   And lete þine sinnes ay and o.
> Do penaunce, fast, and wake,
>   þe fend seyd: 'þou schalt nouʒt so!
> So ʒong þi riot to forsake,
>   And euer to liue in sorwe and wo! "Auch." (ll. 377-384)

The Body has spurned the suggestion of shriving itself and of performing acts of penance, fasting, and watching,

---

[20] St. Thomas Aquinas says the demon's malice makes use of both the world and the flesh in assailing men. *Summa Theologica*, I^a II^{ae}, LXXX, i ad iii.

[21] *Supra*, p. 63, note 5.

The Ethical Meaning of the Analogy

and has given ear to the counsel of the devil. The Soul realizes that the remission of sins requires "schrift of mouth" or confession and also satisfaction.[22] This satisfaction for sin consists in acts of penance, which include prayer and alms, and also fasts.[23] Preaching manuals and sermon books are rich in proof that prayer, alms, and fasting are needful for the sinner who desires to recover his health of soul.[24] These are weapons with which to attack the three foes — the devil, the world, and the flesh — that are the causes of sin in man.[25] Watching, too, is always conjoined with prayer, for when men sleep in deadly sin, they cannot hope that ear be given to prayer.[26] In the above cited passage, for the sake of emphasis, the dreamer injects another voice, that of the fiend. These lines show the devil's method of attack in the soul. Since he is not permitted to attack directly the higher faculties of intellect and will, which God reserves as His own sanctuary,[27] the

---

[22] See St. Thomas Aquinas, *Summa Theologica*, III^a, XC, ii, where he remarks that the material parts of the Sacrament of Penance are contrition, confession, and satisfaction. In *ibid.*, III^a, LXXXIV, iii, he says that the formal part is absolution.

[23] *Ibid.*, III^a, "Supplementum," XV, iii.

[24] See *Twelfth Century Homilies*, p. 46: "Þurh þet festen beoþ þa læhtræs astræhte, þ flæsc biþ ieadmet, þæs deofles costnung oferswiþ [ed.]. ...Witodlice þa festene beoþ stronge iscotu onjean þæs deofles costnunge." Page 44: "Þam reowsijendum witodlice is þeo wæcce to bigánne, forþam þan þe heo to heofenum up ahæfþ þæs reowsiendæn wæstmæs."

[25] See *Old English Homilies*, 53, p. 62; *Early English Homilies*, edited by Rubie D-N. Warner (London: *EETS*, 152, 1917), p. 105.

[26] See *Middle English Sermons*, p. 46: "For þer ben many of vs....þat slepeþ when þei preye....By þis slepe is undirstond dedely synne; for like as a man semeþ dede bodely whan he slepeyþ, ryght so whan a man slepeyþ in dedely synne, vhat good dede þat euere he dothe — preyinge, fastynge, almvs dede doyinge — may ne shall not profitt hym to mede of sowle in þe blisse of heven ne here in vrthe; but he shall haue þe soner grace to rise oute of ys synne." See also *Twelfth Century Homilies*, p. 45.

[27] See St. Thomas Aquinas, *Summa Theologica*, I^a II^{ae}, LXXX, i ad iii: "...quod Deus est universale principium omnis interioris motus humani; sed quod determinetur ad malum consilium voluntas humana, hoc directe quidem est ex voluntate humana, et diabolo per modum persuadentis, vel appetibile proponentis."

devil creeps into man through his senses [28] and acts directly on the imagination and memory, as well as on the passions which reside in the sensitive appetites. The will, however, as Saint Thomas remarks, remains free to give or to refuse consent.[29] Medieval sermons also emphasize the fact that the devil cannot force man. He may only mislead.[30] The Body has yielded to the cunning of the enchanting fiend who has counseled him not to forsake sensual pleasures

>...þou schalt nouȝt so,
>   þus sone al þi blisse forsake, (ll. 268-269)

but to persevere in them since there were still many more years to live.

Again, the Soul, in its own voice, presents the second enemy, the world, which has tempted the Body with worldly pleasures, of which death has robbed it, leaving it naked and bare.

>Ȝwan I bad te leve pride,
>   þi manie mes, þi riche schroud,
>þe false world þat stod biside,
>   Bad þe be ful quoynte and proud;
>þi fleysch with riche robes schride,
>   Nouȝt als a beggare in a clout,
>And on heiȝe horse to ride
>   Wiþ mikel meyne in and out. (ll. 273-280)

The Soul by implication shows that the world has the man-

---

[28] See *Old English Homilies*, 53, p. 34.

[29] *Summa Theologica*, I^a II^{ae}, LXXX, i: "Voluntas autem, sicut supra dictum est, a duobus moveri potest: uno modo ab objecto, sicut dicitur quod appetibile apprehensum movet appetitum; alio modo ab eo quod interius inclinat voluntatem ad volendum; hoc autem non est nisi vel ipsa voluntas, vel Deus, ut supra ostensum est. Deus autem non potest esse causa peccati, ut dictum est. Relinquitur ergo, quod ex hac parte sola voluntas hominis sit directe causa peccati ejus."

[30] "Sermon on the Fourth Sunday after Easter," *Old English Homilies*, 53, p. 104.

ner of deceptive men: those whom it more fondly embraces, on whom it showers the most honors, them it traps the more speedily. This second great enemy of men — the world — urged the Body not to abandon its pride but to take delight in the luxurious life of society, to robe itself in the richest garb, and to continue to ride high on horseback, surrounded by a great retinue. Here is reiterated that extravagant love of life and sensuality which the Soul had previously so deftly outlined in the *Ubi sunt?*, as is seen in chapter I.

Finally, the third adversary is presented — the flesh, which, Saint Thomas declares, is man's own concupiscence.[31]

>3wan I bad þe erliche to rise,
>   Nim of me þi soule kep,
>þou seidest thou miȝtest a none wise
>   Forgon þe mirie morweslep. (ll. 281-284)

Here in these lines is an allusion to the great battle between the senses and reason, and whether the Soul is to be ruled by sin or the Spirit of Life depends on the victory of either the law of members or the law of the mind. This struggle is ever present from the early morning hours on, when the Soul or the law of the mind cries: "Arise, and be on guard for the sake of your soul!" and the law of the flesh cries, "Rest a little longer! Forgo not the merry morning sleep!" On through every hour, almost every moment of the day the tide of the battle ebbs and flows. The Soul makes it clear, by implication, that man must not pamper his flesh which tempts him to gluttony and lechery, for concupiscence smolders in his soul.

With tears the Soul realistically depicts its entanglement in the meshes of the three ghostly adversaries in terms of a timely analogy. The Body, it says, has led it on in its enterprises as a butcher his sheep and his ox.

---

[31] *Summa Theologica*, Iª IIae, LXXXII, i ad iii.

>   ȝe þre traytours, sore I wep;
>   Ye ladde me wiþ ȝoure enprise,
>   As þe bochere doþ his schep. (ll. 286-288)

. . . .

>   ȝe ledde me bi doune and dale
>   As an oxe bi þe horn,
>   Til þer as him is browen bale
>   þer his þrote schal be schorn. (ll. 293-296)

These parallel similes — the sheep led to his natural destruction by the butcher and the ox led by the horns to have its throat slashed — fittingly illustrate how the sorrow-beaten Soul, betrayed into the hands of the devil and the world, has been led to its spiritual destruction by the flesh-loving Body. The sheep and the ox, brute beasts that rate low in the scale of animal alertness, instinctively follow the instruments that direct them to their destruction. In like manner the soul, dispossessed of reason, blindly follows the dictates of its body, ridden by sense-appetite, to its spiritual destruction. The soul like the rider who has lost control of the reins is dragged where the irrational movements of the body carry it.

This enslavement by the infernal enemies draws from the Body a bitter lament over its misspent life. Among other things it bewails the fact that it was fated to be a human Body.

>   ...Allas, þat mi lif hath last,
>   þat I have lived for sinne sake.
>   þat min herte ne hadde tobrast,
>   ȝwan I was fram mi moder take;
>   I miȝte have ben in erþe kast,
>   And leiȝen and roted in a lake.[32] (ll. 315-320)

---

[32] Regretting that one has been born, that one's heart has not been broken at birth, and that one has not been cast to rot in the lake is a commonplace figure in the exemplum. It is also repeated in Wulfstan's Homily XL, "In Die Judicii," in Napier, *op. cit.*, p. 187. In later writings this regret assumes a stronger form, accentuating itself in a cursing of the father and mother that have begotten the individual. See chapter I, note 20. In all other works dealing with the Body-and-Soul legend, these

The above passage and the following

> þanne haved I nevere lerned
>   3wat was yvil, ne 3wat was god,
> Ne no þing with wronge 3ernd,
>   Ne pine þoled as I mot,
> 3were no seint mi3te beren ure ernde
>   To him þat bou3te us with his blod,
> In helle 3wanne we ben bernd
>   Of sum merci to don us bot. (ll. 321-328)

are strongly reminiscent of the third chapter of the Book of Job, especially verses 11-14:

> Why did I not die in the womb? Why did I not perish when I came out of the belly? Why received upon the knees? Why suckled at the breast? For now I should have been asleep and still; and should have rest in my sleep.

There appears in the line — "To him þat bou3te us with his blod," (l. 326) — an allusion to the Redemption, an allusion, clear enough, that has been expounded in many medieval sermons.[33] The Body declares, as the first four lines above indicate, that if it had died before birth, it would never have known evil, nor have trusted the world, nor have suffered as it now must. There is no saint that may intercede with Him who shed His blood, for the time of probation has ended. Both Body and Soul shall burn in hell without mercy.

---

words are put into the mouth of the Soul instead of the Body. The "Auchinleck" text substitutes "Cast into a pit with an adder and a snake" for the *Laud* "and lie and rot in a lake." According to the *NED*, I, 102, *adder* is from the Old English *næddre* and originally meant snake. Whether this is mere poetic repetition or whether there is beginning a modern distinction between the two words, at least to the extent of making *adder* a venomous snake, is not certain.

[33] Compare: Þæt he for ealles macynnes hæle mid his sylfes willan deaþ geþrowode, þeah his þære ecean godcundnesse nænig man sceþþan ne mihte, þæt þe þonne was efne xxxiii wintra...." *Blickling Homilies*, edited by Richard Morris (London: EETS OS, 73, 1880), p. 129.

The Soul quickly interrupts with the assertion that there is no remedy now since the Body has already lost the power of speech (ll. 329-332).

> Ac haddest þou a litel er,
>   ȝwile us was lif togidre lent,
> Þo þat was so sek and ser,
>   Us schriven and þe devel schent,
> And laten renne a reuly ter,
>   And bihiȝt amendement,
> Ne þorte us have friȝt ne fer,
>   Þat God ne wolde us blisse have sent. (ll. 337-344)

The Soul as inward mentor suggests the procedure which should have been followed to avert eternal punishment. It exhorts the Body with the reminder that if it had shriven itself, foiled the devil, and made satisfaction for sin, while it lay sick unto death when Body and Soul were alive and one, God would have granted mercy and averted punishment. Prayers are of no avail now, because the Soul is damned.[34]

> Þeiȝ alle þe men nou under mone
>   To demen weren sete on benche,
> Þe schames þat us schullen be done
>   Ne schulden halven del biþenche.
> Ne helpeþ us no bede ne bone,
>   Ne may us nou no wyl towrenche; (ll. 305-310)

Though all the people in this world were placed in a seat of judgment, they could not possibly imagine half the ignominy that shall await Body and Soul. Prayers and boons are useless for the eternally lost. The poet empha-

---

[34] Suffrages do not profit the damned, nor does the Church intend to pray for them. See St. Thomas Aquinas, *Summa Theologica*, III^a, *Supplementum*, LXXI, v.

sizes this by placing the following additional stanza in the mouth of the Soul.

> Þey alle þe men þat ben o lyve
>   Weren prestes, messes for to singe,
> And alle þe maidenes and þe wyve
>   Wydewes, hondene for to wringe,
> And miȝte sweche fyve
>   Als is in werld of alle þinge,
> Siþin we ne mouwen us selven schrive,
>   Ne schulde us into blisse bringe. (ll. 345-352)

Even if all the men in the world were to say Masses and all the women were to wring their hands in prayer; and even if this number were multiplied by five, salvation would not be possible, since there is no time for repentance. The benefits of the Mass, though infinite in value, are powerless for a Soul that has been damned.[85]

It is to be understood that the Body-and-Soul theme deals only with the fortunes of the soul and body immediately after death has separated them and has nothing to do with the final judgment at the end of the world, when Jesus shall return and shall definitely fix the state of man. Medieval writers were not always able to keep the two separated. Medieval interest lay chiefly in what follows afterwards, in the final episode depicted in *The Debate between the Body and the Soul,* in the pains of hell.

The problem of the future fortune of the Soul and Body is approached, as one would expect, by the Soul.

> Of alle dedes thou didest ille
>   Þat þou so liȝtli schalt be quite? (ll. 71-72)

---

[85] In the light of the stanza quoted, it can hardly be argued, then, as Mabel Stanford has argued, that the poet makes hell "as vivid as possible," with the obvious motive of stirring people to give money for Masses. "Sumnour's Tale," *JEGP,* XIX (1920), 380. It seems more likely that the poet's purpose was to urge readers to lead a good life so that they might escape going to hell.

The Body cannot hope to escape lightly, since it, too, has done ill; therefore, it must be punished.

> Wenest ou nou to gete þe griþ
> þer þou list roten in þe clay?
> þey þou be rotin pile and piþ,
> And blowen wiþ þe wind away,
> Ʒet schalt ou come wiþ lime and lyþ
> Agein to me on domesday,
> And come to court and I þe wiþ
> For to kepen oure harde pay. (ll. 73-80)

The Soul, indignant at the Body's argument that it was merely to serve the Soul (ll. 57-60), as was mentioned previously, retorts that the Body will not lie rotting in the grave until its ashes are blown away by the wind; but on Doomsday both shall come to judgment where each shall receive a just recompense. The Soul compares the judgment with a court of justice where the plaintiff and defendant, Soul and Body, will present their good and bad deeds on reckoning day at the end of the world. This comparison is in accord with the poet's conception of Christ as seated on a throne (ll. 443-444) and of hell as a dungeon or a prison (l. 472).

There is another implicit reference to the judgment in the thought that many have gone to the grave and this fact should have been a warning to the Body.

> þou was warned her bifore,
> Ʒwat we boþe scholden have;
> Idel tale held tou þat þore
> þou sauʒ fele dun in grave. (ll. 201-204)

The Soul's own words that it possesses a knowledge of its own fate immediately after death give testimony to the poet's belief in a particular judgment.

Bodi, I may no more dwelle,
 Ne stonde for to speke with þe;
Hellehoundes here I ȝelle,
 And fendes mo þan men mowe se,
Þat comen to fette me to helle,
 Ne may I noȝwer from hem fle;
And þou schalt comen with fleys and felle
 A domesday to wone with me. (ll. 353-360)

In the passage under discussion the Soul apparently has still more to say to the Body — "Ne stonde for to speke" — but the hell-horde is already present to fetch it to hell. It has already received its assignment, where it will remain temporarily without the Body, but at the general judgment the entire Body, "fleys and felle," will come to judgment with the Soul.

Preceding the general judgment, when the souls are judged in union with their bodies on Doomsday, is the particular judgment. This judgment is instantaneous, contemporary theologians supposed, for in the moment of death the separated soul is internally illuminated as to its own guilt or innocence and of its own initiative takes its course to either hell or purgatory or heaven.[36]

Through the rider-and-horse analogy the poet has shown how man's rational life, the excellent part of his nature, must control the irrational life. Just as the rider draws in his reins to control the fleet steed, the soul must curb the non-rational appetites that constantly strive to gain the upper hand. Closely related to this image is the master-and-servant analogy whereby the poet points out that the soul in order to be a wise governor and protector must remain a faithful servant of God. It is the sad burden of the soul, however, that though it ought to be a servant of God, its very government over the body can attract it to the

---

[36] St. Thomas says that as soon as the soul is set free from the body, it is assigned a place in keeping with its reward or punishment. *Summa Theologica*, IIIa, "Supplementum," LXIX, ii. See also *ibid.*, LXXXVIII, ii, for a discussion of the General Judgment.

point of becoming its servant. In *The Debate between the Body and the Soul* the servant has gained mastery over the ruler; the horse has run away with the bridle; the body has entangled the soul in its meshes and has seduced it to sin. It is with the devil and the world that the body has leagued itself and conspired against the soul, the three constituting the unholy trinity of man's traditional enemies.

CHAPTER IV

CONCLUSION

The image of the horse and the horseman has had a long history. It appeared in the writings of men, such as pseudo-Trismegistus, Philo Judæus, Plutarch, Varro, Saint John Chrysostom, and Saint Augustine, and became a commonplace in medieval religious writings. Historically, the function of the image has been twofold. Writers employed it either to express the notion of the relationship existing between the body and the soul in terms of the essence of man, or to show that the soul, the seat of the intellect and will, bears the responsibility of controlling man's actions.

A study of the analogy of the horse and rider and of the metaphor, *life's light*, reveals that the poet of *The Debate between the Body and the Soul*, either consciously or unconsciously, followed the Platonic path traveled by Saint Augustine, Hugh of St. Victor, Robert Grosseteste, and the author of the pseudo-Augustinian treatise, *De Spiritu et Anima*. According to them the emphasis in defining human nature was put on the soul to the extent of ultimately making the soul the true man and considering the body merely as an organ of the soul, not as an essential constituent of the whole man. In this, *The Debate* is in conflict with Thomistic teaching, which posits a real union between the body and the soul.

Inasmuch as the body possessed the powers of locomotion, sight, hearing, nutrition as companion of the soul, it may be concluded that the poet identified the powers of the soul with its very essence. Most writers who influenced medieval thinking, such as Saint Augustine, Gregory the Great, Isidore of Seville, Alcuin, Rhaban Maurus, William of St. Thierry, William of Auvergne, followed Saint Augustine and did not distinguish between the soul and its operations.

The context of the poem also reveals that sensations are but operations of the soul through the bodily organism. In the doctrine of Saint Thomas sensation cannot be considered an act of the soul alone but must be explained as belonging to the composite man. It is impossible to explain sensation as a human activity if it takes place in a body which is joined to the soul only after the fashion of a horse to a rider or a motor to a boat. If the soul and body are not one in *esse* they cannot be one in operation.[1]

The poet, in harmony with the teaching of Saint Thomas, places the knowledge of right and wrong and the responsibility for conduct in the soul. Saint Thomas declares that every act of the will depends upon the act of the intellect, since the will becomes active only when the cognitive faculty presents an object to it. Knowledge by its guidance and direction and will by its command unite in action to effect a common result. But Saint Thomas also declares that in every thought, in every action, man uses the material body inasmuch as its activity supplies the phantasm. Where sensation is an act of the soul alone, the body cannot function as Saint Thomas would require.

But a consideration of the horse-and-rider image as the poet would have it function metaphorically in the poem reveals the soul as having taken up its abode in the breast of the bodily frame and from there ruling and guiding the body. The poet relates the body to a horse which the soul as rider cannot govern and shows how the soul, once it has lost control of its irrational nature, is dragged by the unruly passions to the level of the brute just as the rider who has lost the reins of the horse is dragged wherever the irrational movements of the horse carry him. In the image is implied the poet's awareness of the irregularity in the soul, the struggle between the law of the members and the law of the mind, the tendency to evil inherited by every man from Adam, and this same inclination intensified by man's sins and vices.

---

[1] St. Thomas Aquinas, *Summa Theologica*, I^a, LXXV, iv, *Resp.*

In harmony with the horse-and-rider image is the metaphor of the master and the servant. The master like the rider has the power of control, guidance, and protection while the servant like the horse exerts himself for his master. But the more the body seeks the protection of the soul, the more the soul becomes implicated in its care; and the more the soul becomes implicated in its care, it stays to enjoy where it should have stayed to rule. The master also rules the servant by a force which the servant has no power to contradict, for when he is told to go, he goes. But the rider cannot expect such obedience from a horse; he must make the horse do as he wishes by using the bridle. In like manner the faculty of man's exterior motion never fails to obey. His sense and faculties of nourishing, growing, producing, however, he must manage with industry and art, because man cannot govern these with the same ease as exterior motion.

By means of the horse-and-rider analogy, together with the metaphor of the servant and the master and other related images, the poet concretizes the activities of the flesh and its betrayal of the soul into the hands of the two other members of the unholy trinity, the world and the devil. The soul having lost control of its irrational nature was dragged by the unruly passions to its spiritual death. The responsibility for the loss of the soul rests, therefore, with the soul since it was assigned the direction of the body.

APPENDIX

THE DEBATE BETWEEN THE BODY AND THE SOUL [1]

Als I lay in a winteris nyʒt
  In a droupening bifor þe day,
Forsoþe I sauʒ a selly syʒt,
  A body on a bere lay,
þat havede ben a mody knyʒt
  And litel served God to pay;
Loren he haved þe lives lyʒt,
  þe gost was oute and scholde away.

Wan þe gost it scholde go,
  It biwente and withstod,
Biheld the body þere it cam fro
  So serfulli with dredli mod;
It seide, 'Weile and walawo!
  Wo worþe þi fleys, þi foule blod.
Wreche bodi wʒy list ou so,
  þat ʒwilene were so wilde and wod?

'þou þat were woned to ride
  Heyʒe on horse in and out,
So kweynte kniʒt ikuþ so wide,
  As a lyun fers and proud,
ʒwere is al þi michele pride,
  And þi lede þat was so loud?
ʒwi list ou þere so bare o side
  Ipricked in þat pore schroud?

---

[1] *A Middle English Reader*, edited by O. F. Emerson (London: Macmillan, 1905), pp. 47-64. Reprinted by permission of Macmillan and Company, Ltd., London.

'Ȝwere ben þi wurþli wedes,
    þi somers with þi riche beddes,
þi proude palefreys and þi stedes?
    þat þou about in dester leddes?
þi faucouns þat were wont to grede,
    And þine houndes þat þou fedde?
Me þinkeþ God is þe to gnede,
    þat alle þine frend beon fro þe fledde.

'Ȝwere beon þi castles and þi toures,
    þi chaumbres and þi riche halles
Ipeynted with so riche floures,
    And þi riche robes alle?
þine cowltes and þi covertoures,
    þi cendels and þi riche palles?
Wreche, ful derk is nou þi bour;
    Tomoruwe þou schalt þerinne falle.

'Ȝwere ben þine cokes snelle,
    þat scholden gon to greiþe þi mete
With speces swete for to smelle,
    þat þou nevere were fol of frete,
To do þat foule fleys to swelle
    þat foule wormes scholden ete?
And þou havest þe pine of helle
    With glotonye me bigete....'

'For God þe schop aftir his schaft,
    And gaf þe boþe wyt and skil;
In þi loking was I laft
    To wisse aftir þin oune wil.
Ne toc I nevere wychecraft,
    Ne wist I ȝwat was god nor il,
Bote as a wretche dumb and daft,
    Bote as tou taugtest me þertil.

'Set to serven þe to queme
  Boþe at even and at morn,
Siþin I was þe bitauȝt to ȝeme,
  Fro þe time þat þou was born.
Þou þat dedes couþest deme
  Scholdest habbe be war biforn
Of mi folye, as it seme;
  Nou wiþ þiselve thou art forlorn.'

Þe gast it seyde, 'Bodi be stille!
  Ȝwo haþ lered þe al þis wite
Þat givest me þese wordes grille,
  Þat list þer bollen as a bite?
Wenest ou, wretche, þoȝ thou fille
  Wiþ þi foule fleisch a pite,
Of alle dedes thou didest ille
  Þat þou so liȝtli schalt be quite?

'Wenest ou nou to gete þe griþ
  Þer þou list roten in þe clay?
Þey þou be rotin pile and piþ,
  And blowen wiþ þe wind away,
Ȝet schalt ou come wiþ lime and lyþ
  Agein to me on domesday,
And come to court and I þe wiþ
  For to kepen oure harde pay.

'To teche were þou me bitauȝt;
  Ac ȝwan þou þouȝtest of þe qued,
Wiþ þi teþ þe bridel þou lauȝt,
  Þou dist al þat I þe forbed.
To sinne and schame it was þi drauȝt,
  Til untid and til wikkedehed;
Inouȝ I stod ageyn and fauȝt,
  Bot ai þou nome þin oune red.

'Wan I þe wolde teme and teche
    ȝwat was yvel and ȝwat was god,
Of Crist ne kirke was no speche,
    Bote renne aboute and breyde wod;
Inouȝ I miȝte preye and preche,
    Ne miȝte I nevere wende þi mod
Þat þou woldest God knouleche,
    But don al þat þin herte to stod.

'I bad þe þenke on soulenedes,
    Matines, masse, and evesong;
Thou mostist first don oþere dedes,
    Þou seidist al was idel gong.
To wode and water and feld thou edest,
    Or to court to do men wrong;
Bote for pride or grettore medes
    Litel þou dist god among.

'Ho may more trayson do,
    Or his loverd betere engine,
Þan he þat al his trist is to,
    In and out as oune hyn?
Ay seþþe þou was þriven and þro,
    Miȝtis did I alle mine,
To porveie þe rest and ro,
    And þou to bringe me in pine.

'Nou mouwe þe wilde bestes renne
    And lien under linde and lef,
And foules flie bi feld and fenne,
    Siþin þi false herte clef.
Þine eiȝene are blinde and connen nouȝt kenne,
    Þi mouth is dumb, þin ere is def;
And nou so loþli þou list grenne
    Fro þe comeþ a wikke wef.

'Ne nis no levedi briȝt on ble,
   þat wel were woned of þe to lete,
þat wolde lye a niȝt bi þe
   For nouȝt þat men miȝte hem bihete.
þou art unsemly for to se,
   Uncomli for to kissen swete;
þou ne havest frend þat ne wolde fle,
   Come þou stertlinde in þe strete.'

þe bodi it seide, 'Ic seyȝe,
   Gast, þou hast wrong iwys
Al þe gilt on me to leyȝe,
   þat þou hast lorn þi mikil blis.
Were was I bi wode or weyȝe,
   Sat or stod or dide ouȝt mys,
þat I ne was ay under þin eyȝe?
   Wel þou wost þat soth it is.

'Wedir I ede up or doun,
   þat I ne bar þe on my bac,
Als þin as fro toun to toun,
   Alse þou me lete have rap and rac?
þat tou ne were and rede roun
   Nevere did I þing ne spac;
Here þe soþe se men mowen
   On me þat ligge so blo and blac.

'For al þe wile þou were mi fere
   I hadde al þat me was ned,
I miȝte speke, se and here,
   I ede and rod and drank and et.
Loþli chaunged is my chere
   Sin þe tyme þat þou me let;
Def and dumb I ligge on bere,
   þat I ne may sterin hand ne fet.

'I scholde have ben dumb as a schep,
   Or as an ouwe or as a swyn
þat et and drank and lai and slep,
   Slayn, and passid al his pin;
Nevere of catel nome kep,
   Ne wyste wat was water ne wyn,
Ne leyn in helle þat is so dep,
   Ne were þe wit þat al was þin.'

Þe gast it seide, 'Is no doute;
   Abouten, bodi, þou me bar;
Þou mostist nede, I was wiþoute
   Hand and fot, I was wel war.
Bote as tou bere me aboute
   Ne miȝt I do þe leste char;
Þorfore most I nede loute,
   So doth þat non oþer dar.

'Of o wymman born and bredde,
   Body, were we boþe two;
Togidre fostrid fayre and fedde
   Til þou couþist speke and go.
Softe þe for love I ledde,
   Ne dorst I nevere do þe wo;
To lese þe so sore I dredde,
   And wel I wiste to gete na mo.

For me þou woldest sumwat do
   Wȝile þou were ȝong a litil first,
For frendes eyȝe þat þe stod to,
   Þe wile þou were betin and birst;
Oc wan þou were þriven and þro,
   And knewe hunger, cold and þirst,
And ȝhwilk was eyse, rest and ro,
   Al þin oune wil þou dist.

'I saw þe fair on fleysch and blod
    And al mi love on þe I kest;
þat þou þrive me þouȝte god,
    And let þe haven ro and rest.
þat made þe so stirne of mod,
    And of werkes so unwrest;
To fiȝte with þe ne was no bot
    Me þat þou bar in þi brest.

'Gloterie and lecherie,
    Pride and wicke coveytise,
Niþe and onde and envie
    To God of hevene and alle hise,
And in unlust for to lye,
    Was ti wone in alle wise;
That I schal nou ful dere abye,
    A, weyle! sore may me grise.

'þou was warned her bifore,
    Ȝwat we boþe scholden have;
Idel tale held tou þat þore
    þou sauȝ fele dun in grave.
þou dist al þat þe werld þe bad,
    And þat þi fleys þe wolde crave;
I þolede þe and dide as mad
    To be maister and I þi cnave.'

'Iwenest þou, gost, þe geyned ouȝt
    For to quite þe wiþal,
þou þat was so worþli wrouȝt,
    To seye I made þe my þral?
Did I nevere on live nouȝt,
    I ne rafte ne I ne stal
þat first of þe ne cam þe þouȝt;
    Aby it þat abyȝe schal!

'3wat wist I wat was wrong or riht,
    Wat to take or 3wat to schone,
Bote þat þou pottest in mi si3ht
    þat al þe wisdom scholdest cone?
3wanne þou me tau3tist on unti3ht,
    And me gan þeroffe mone,
þanne did I al my mi3ht
    Anoþer time to have my wone.

'Oc haddist þou, þat Crist it ouþe,
    Given me honger, þirst and cold,
And þou witest me þat no god couþe,
    In bismere 3wan I was so bold,
þat I hadde undernomen in 3ouþe
    I havede holden 3wan I was old,
þou let me reykin north and south
    And haven al my wille on wold.

'þou scholdist for no lif ne lond,
    Ne for non oþer worldes winne,
Have soffrid me to lein on hond,
    þat havede tornd to schame or sinne
Oc for I þe so eise fond,
    And þi wretche wit so þinne,
þat ay was wriþinde as a wond,
    þerfore couþe I nevere blinne.

'To sinne þou wistist was my kinde,
    As mankinne it is al so,
And to þe wretche world so minde,
    And to þe fend þat is ure fo.
þou scholdest er have late me binde
    Wan I misdede, and don me wo;
Ac 3wanne þe blinde lat þe blinde,
    In dike he fallen boþe two.'

Tho bigan þe gost to wepe,
    And seide, 'Bodi, allas, allas,
þat I þe lovede evere ȝete,
    For al mi love on þe I las.
þat tou lovedest me þou lete,
    And madest me an houve of glas;
I dide al þat þe was sete,
    And þou my traytor evere was.

'þe fend of helle þat haveþ envie
    To mankinne, and evere haþ had,
Was in us as is a spie
    To do sum god ȝwan I þe bad.
The werld he toc to cumpaynie,
    þat mani a soule haved forrad;
þey þre wisten þi folye,
    And maden, wretche, þe al mad.

'Ȝwan I bad þe reste take,
    Forsake sinne ay and oo,
Do penaunce, faste and wake,
    þe fend seide, 'þou schalt nouȝt so,
þus sone al þi blisse forsake,
    To liven ay in pine and wo!
Joye and blisse I rede þou make,
    And þenke to live ȝeres mo.

'Ȝwan I bad te leve pride,
    þi manie mes, þi riche schroud,
þe false world þat stod biside,
    Bad þe be ful quoynte and proud;
þi fleysch with riche robes schride,
    Nouȝt als a beggare in a clout,
And on heiȝe horse to ride
    Wiþ mikel meyne in and out.

'Ȝwan I bad þe erliche to rise,
  Nim of me þi soule kep,
Þou seidest thou miȝtest a none wise
  Forgon þe mirie morweslep.
Wȝan ȝe hadden set your sise,
  Ȝe þre traytours, sore I wep;
Ye ladde me wiþ ȝoure enprise,
  As þe bochere doþ his schep.

'Ȝwan ȝe þre traitours at o tale
  Togidere weren agein me sworn,
Al ȝe maden trotevale
  Þat I haved seid biforn.
Ȝe ledde me bi doune and dale
  As an oxe bi þe horn,
Til þer as him is browen bale
  Þer his þrote schal be schorn.

'For love þe wille I folewede al,
  And to min oune deth I drouȝ,
To foluwe þe þat was mi þral,
  Þat evere were false and frouȝ;
Þou it dist and I forhal,
  We wisten wel it was wouȝ;
Þerfore mote we kepe ure fal,
  Pine and schame and sorewe inouȝ.

'Þeiȝ alle þe men nou under mone
  To demen weren sete on benche,
Þe schames þat us schullen be done
  Ne schulden halven del biþenche.
Ne helpeþ us no bede ne bone,
  Ne may us nou no wyl towrenche;
Hellehoundes comen nou sone,
  Forþi ne mouwe we noyþer blenche.'

3wan þat bodi say þat gast
    þat mone and al þat soruwe make,
It seide, 'Allas, þat mi lif hath last,
    þat I have lived for sinne sake.
þat min herte ne hadde tobrast,
    3wan I was fram mi moder take;
I mi3te have ben in erþe kast,
    And lei3en and roted in a lake.

'þanne haved I nevere lerned
    3wat was yvil, ne 3wat was god,
Ne no þing with wronge 3ernd,
    Ne pine þoled as I mot,
3were no seint mi3te beren ure ernde
    To him þat bou3te us with his blod,
In helle 3wanne we ben bernd
    Of sum merci to don us bot.

'Nay, bodi, nay, nou is to late
    For to preien and to preche,
Nou þe wayn is atte 3ate,
    And þi tonge haþ leid þe speche.
O poynt of ure pine to bate,
    In þe world ne is no leche;
Al tegidere we gon o gate,
    Swilk is Godes harde wreche.

'Ac haddest þou a litel er,
    3wile us was lif togidre lent,
Þo þat was so sek and ser,
    Us schriven and þe devel schent,
And laten renne a reuly ter,
    And bihi3t amendement,
Ne þorte us have fri3t ne fer,
    þat God ne wolde us blisse have sent.

'Þey alle þe men þat ben o lyve
    Weren prestes, messes for to singe,
And alle þe maidenes and þe wyve
    Wydewes, hondene for to wringe,
And miȝte sweche fyve
    Als is in werld of alle þinge,
Siþin we ne mouwen us selven schrive,
    Ne schulde us into blisse bringe.

'Bodi, I may no more dwelle,
    Ne stonde for to speke with þe;
Hellehoundes here I ȝelle,
    And fendes mo þan men mowe se,
Þat comen to fette me to helle,
    Ne may I noȝwer from hem fle;
And þou schalt comen with fleys and felle
    A domesday to wone with me.'

Ne havede it nou er þe word iseyd,
    It ne wiste ȝwider it scholde go;
In abreken at a breid
    A þousend develene and ȝet mo.
Ȝwan thei hadden on him leyd
    Here scharpe cloches alle þo,
It was in a sori pleyt,
    Reuliche toyled to and fro.

For thei weren ragged, roue and tayled,
    With brode bulches on here bac;
Scharpe clauwes, longe nayled,
    No was no lime withoute lac.
On alle halve it was asayled
    With mani a devel foul and blac;
Merci criende litel availede
    Ȝwan Crist it wolde so harde wrac.

Some þe chaules it towraste
    And ȝoten in þe led al hot,
And bedin him to drinke faste,
    And shenke abouten him abrot.
A devil kam þer atte laste
    þat was maister, wel I wot;
A colter glowende in him he þraste
    þat it þoruȝ þe herte smot.

Gleyves glowende some setten
    To bac and brest and boþe sides,
þat in his herte þe poyntes mettin,
    And maden him þo woundes wide,
And seiden him fol wel he lette
    þe herte þat was so fol of pride;
Wel he it hadde þat men him hette,
    For more scholde it bitide.

Worþli wedes for to were
    þei seiden þat he lovede best;
A develes cope for to bere,
    Al brennynde on him was kest,
With hote haspes imad to spere
    þat streite sat to bac and brest;
An helm þat was litel to here
    Kam him, and an hors al prest.

Forth was brouȝt þerewith a bridel,
    A corsed devel als a cote,
þat grisliche grennede and ȝenede wide,
    þe leyȝe it lemede of his þrote;
With a sadel to the midside
    Fol of scharpe pikes schote,
Alse an hechele on to ride;
    Al was glowende, ilke a grote.

Upon þat sadil he was sloungen,
    As he scholde to þe tornement;
An hundred devel on him dongen
    Her and þer þan he was hent;
With hote speres þoruʒ was stongen,
    And wiþ oules al torent;
At ilke dint þe sparkles sprongen
    As of a brond þat were forbrent.

ʒwan he hadde riden þat rode
    Upon þe sadil þer he was set,
He was kast doun as a tode,
    And hellehoundes to him were let
þat broiden out þo peces brode,
    Als he to helle ward was fet;
Ther alle þe fendes fet it trode,
    Men miʒte of blod foluwe þe tred.

He beden him honten and blowen,
    Crien on Bauston and Bewis,
þe ratches þat him were woned to knowen
    He scholden sone blowe þe pris;
An hundred develes, on a rowe,
    With stringes him drowen, unþanc his,
Til he kome to þat loþli lowe
    þer helle was, I wot to wis.

ʒwan it kam to þat wikke won,
    þe fendes kasten swilk a ʒel,
þe erþe it openede anon,
    Smoke and smoþer up it wel;
Boþe of pich and of brimston,
    Men myʒte fif mile have þe smel.
Loverd, wo schal him be bigon
    þat haþ þeroffe þe tenþe del!

Ȝwan þe gost þe soþe isey,
  Wȝider it scholde, it kaste a cri,
And seide, 'Jesu that sittest on hey,
  On me, þi schap, nou have merci.
Ne schope þou me þat are so slyȝ?
  þi creature al so was I
Als man þat sittes þe so nyȝ,
  þat þou havest so wel don by.

'þou þat wistest al biforn,
  Wȝi schope þou me to wroþer hele,
To be þus togged and totorn,
  And oþere to haven al mi wele?
þo þat scholden be forlorn,
  Wretches þat tou miȝtest spele,
A, weile, wȝi lest ou hem be born,
  To ȝeve þe foule fend so fele?'

Agein him þe fendes gonnen crie,
  'Caitif, helpeþ þe na more
To calle on Jesus ne Marie,
  Ne to crie Cristes ore.
Loren þou havest the cumpainye,
  þou havest served us so ȝore;
þarfore nou þou schalt abye
  As oþere þat leven on ure lore.'

þe foule fendes þat weren fayn,
  Bi top and tail he slongen hit,
And kesten it with myȝt and mayn
  Doun into the develes pit,
þer sonne ne schal nevere be seyn;
  Hemself he sonken in þermit;
þe erþe himself it lek aȝeyn,
  Anon þe donge it was fordit.

Wȝan it was forth, þat foule lod
    To hellewel or it were day,
On ilk a her a drope stod
    For friȝt and fer þer as I lay;
To Jesu Crist with milde mod
    Ȝerne I kalde and lokede ay,
Ȝwan þo fendes hot and wod
    Come to fette me away.

I þonke him þat þolede deth,
    His michele merci and his ore,
þat schilde me fram mani a qued,
    A sinful man as I lai þore.
Þo alle sinful I rede hem red
    To shriven hem and rewen sore;
Nevere was sinne idon so gret
    þat Cristes merci ne is wel more.

BIBLIOGRAPHY

MEDIEVAL TEXTS — VERNACULAR

Berners, Dame Juliana. *The Boke of St. Albans.* London: Elliot Stock, 1901.

Blickling Homilies of the Tenth Century. Edited by Richard Morris. London: *EETS OS*, 58, 1874.

Blickling Homilies. Edited by Richard Morris. London: *EETS OS*, 73, 1880.

Brown, Carleton (ed.). *English Lyrics of the Thirteenth Century.* Oxford: Clarendon Press, 1932.

Buchholz, Richard (ed.). *Die Fragmente der Reden der Seele an den Leichnam. Erlanger Beiträge zur Englischen Philologie,* Bd. I (1890), Heft VI.

Early English Homilies. Edited by Rubie D-N. Warner. London: *EETS*, 152, 1917.

Emerson, Oliver (ed.). *A Middle English Reader.* London: Macmillan, 1905.

Erthe Upon Erthe. Edited by Hilda M. R. Murray. London: *EETS OS*, 141, 1911.

Förster, Max (ed.). *Die Vercelli Homilien, Bibliothek der Angelsächsischen Prosa,* XII. Hamburg, 1932.

Furnivall, Frederick J. (ed.). *Minor Poems of the Vernon MS.* Part II. London: *EETS OS*, 117, 1901.

Hoccleve, Thomas. *Regement of Princes and Fourteen Minor Poems.* Edited by Frederick J. Furnivall. London: *EETS ES*, 72, 1897.

Horstman, Carl (ed.). *Yorkshire Writers: Richard Rolle of Hampole and His Followers.* New York: The Macmillan Company, 1896. Volume II.

———. *Minor Poems of the Vernon MS.* Part I. London: *EETS OS*, 98, 1892.

———. *Early South English Legendary.* London: *EETS OS*, 87, 1887.

Jacob's Well. An Englisht Treatise on the Cleansing of Man's Conscience. Edited by Arthur Brandeis. London: *EETS OS*, 115, 1900.

Krapp, George. *The Vercelli Book. The Anglo-Saxon Poetic Records,* II. New York: Columbia University Press, 1932.

Layamon. *Brut or Chronicle of Britain.* Edited by Sir Frederic Madden. London: Society of Antiquaries, 1847. Volume II.

Linow, Wilhelm, *þe Desputisoun bitwen þe Bodi and þe Soule*. *Erlanger Beiträge zur Englischen Philologie* (1889), Part I, 24-195.

Mankind. *Chief Pre-Shakespearean Dramas*. Edited by Joseph Quincy Adams. Boston: Houghton Mifflin Company, 1924, pp. 304-324.

Middle English Sermons. Edited by Woodburn O. Ross. London: *EETS OS*, 209, 1940.

Morton, James (ed.). *The Ancren Riwle*. London: Printed for the Camden Society, 1853.

Myrc, John. *Festial*. Edited by Theodor Erbe. London: *EETS OS*, 96, 1905.

Napier, A. S. (ed.). *Wulfstan. Sammlung der ihm zugeschriebenen Homilien nebst Untersuchungen über ihre Echtheit*. Berlin: Weidmann, 1883.

Old English Homilies. Edited by Richard Morris. London: *EETS OS*, 29, 1867.

Old English Homilies of the Tenth and Twelfth Centuries. Edited by Richard Morris. London: *EETS OS*, 34, 1868.

Old English Homilies of the Twelfth Century. London: *EETS OS*, 53, 1873.

Old English Miscellany. Edited by Richard Morris. London: *EETS OS*, 49, 1872.

Pricke of Conscience. Edited by Richard Morris. Berlin: A. Ascher, 1863.

Skelton, John. *Magnyfycence*. Edited by Robert Lee Ramsay. London: *EETS ES*, 98, 1906.

Speculum Sacerdotale. Edited by Edward H. Weatherly. London: *EETS OS*, 200, 1936.

Story of Genesis and Exodus. Edited by Richard Morris. London: *EETS OS*, 7, 1865.

Thorpe, B. *Homilies of the Anglo-Saxon Church*. Oxford: Aelfric Society, 1844-1846. Volume I.

———. *Ancient Laws and Institutes of England*. Folio Edition. London: G. E. Eyre and Spottiswoode, 1849.

Turnbull, W. B. *The Vision of Tundale*. Edited by Thomas Stevenson. Edinburgh: 87 Princes Street, 1843.

Twelfth Century Homilies. Edited by A. O. Belfour. Part I. London: *EETS OS*, 137, 1909.

General

Allen, Beatrice. "The Debate of the Body and Soul in MS Digby 86, Miscellaneous Notes." *MLR*, XXII (1927), 189.

Allison, Tempe. "On the Body and the Soul Legend in the *Castle of Perseverance, MLN*, XLII (1927), 102-106.

Batiouchkof, Thomas. "Le Debat de l'Ame et du Corps." *Romania*, XX (1891), 1-55; 513-578.

Baumgartner, M. *Die Philosophie des Alanus de Insulis, BGPM*, II, 4. Münster: Aschendorf, 1896.

Becker, E. *A Contribution to the Comparative Study of the Medieval Visions of Heaven and Hell*. Ph.D. Dissertation. Johns Hopkins University. Baltimore: John Murphy, 1899.

Bourke, Vernon. *Augustine's Quest of Wisdom*. Milwaukee: The Bruce Publishing Company, 1945.

Brennan, Robert, O.P. *The History of Psychology*. New York: The Macmillan Company, 1946.

Brown, Carleton. *A Register of Middle English Religious and Didactic Verse*. Oxford: Clarendon Press, 1920. Volume II.

Capellanus, Andreas. *The Art of Courtly Love*. Translated by John Jay Parry. New York: Columbia University Press, 1941.

Collins, Sister Emmanuel, O.S.F., "Debat." *Dictionary of World Literature*. Edited by Joseph T. Shipley. New York: Philosophical Library, 1943.

Coogan, Sister Mary Philippa, B.V.M. *An Interpretation of the Moral Play, "Mankind."* Ph.D. Dissertation. The Catholic University of America. Washington: The Catholic University of America Press, 1947.

Cooke, Bernard, S.J. "The Mutability-Immutability Principle in St. Augustine's Metaphysics." *The Modern Schoolman*, XIII (1946), 175-193.

Dante, A. *The Divine Comedy*. Translated by Henry F. Cary. New York: P. F. Collier, 1901.

Demers, G. Ed. "Les divers sens du mot Ratio au Moyen Age," *Etudes d'Histoire Litteraire et Doctrinale du XIII*e *Siècle*. Ottawa: Insti. d'Etudes Medievales, 1932. Premiere series.

De Wulf, Maurice. *History of Medieval Philosophy*. Translated by E. C. Messenger. Third English Edition. New York: Longmans, Green and Company, 1935. Volume II.

———. *History of Medieval Philosophy*. Translated by P. Coffey. New York: Longmans, Green and Company, 1909.

———. *Scholasticism Old and New.* Translated by P. Coffey. London: Longmans, Green and Company. No Date.

Didron, Adolphe. *Christian Iconography or The History of Art in the Middle Ages.* Translated by J. Millington. London: George Bell and Sons, 1886. Volume I.

Dudley, Louise. *The Egyptian Elements in the Legend of the Body and Soul.* Bryn Mawr College Monographs, No. 8. Baltimore: Furst, 1911.

Edward the Second, Duke of York. *The Master of Game. The Oldest English Book on Hunting.* Edited by Wm. A. and F. Baillie-Grohman. New York: Ballantyne and Hanson, 1909.

Gasquet, Abbot. *Parish Life in Medieval England.* London: Metheun, 1907.

Gilson, Etienne. *Les Idees et les lettres.* Paris: Librairie Philosophique de la Sorbonne, 6, 1932.

———. *The Philosophy of St. Bonaventure.* Translated by Illtyd Trethowan. New York: Sheed and Ward, 1938.

Hanford, James H. "Debate of the Heart and Eye." *MLN*, XXVI (1911), 161-165.

Heesch, J. *Ueber Sprache und Versbau des halbsächsischen Gedichts, "þe Desputisoun bitwen þe Bodi and þe Soule."* Kieler Dissertation: Kiel, 1884.

Henningham, Eleanor. "Old English Predecessors of the *Worcester Fragments*," *PMLA*, LV (1940), 291-307.

———. (ed.). *An Early Latin Debate of the Body and the Soul. Preserved in MS Royal 7 A III in British Museum.* Ph.D. Dissertation. New York University. New York: Published Privately, 1939.

Holmes, Urban T. *A History of Old French Literature.* New York: F. S. Crofts, 1937.

Huizinga, Jacob. *The Waning of the Middle Ages.* London: E. Arnold, 1924.

Keeler, Leo, S.J. "The Dependence of Robert R. Grosseteste's *De Anima* on the *Summa* of Philip the Chancellor," *The New Scholasticism*, XI (1937), 197-219.

Ker, W. P. *Epic and Romance: Essays on Medieval Literature.* London: Macmillan, 1931.

Kirby, Thomas. *Chaucer's Troilus: A Study in Courtly Love.* University: Louisiana State University Press, 1940.

Kluge, F. "Zu Altenglischen Dichtungen, 2. Nochmals der Seefahrer." *Englische Studien*, VIII (1885), 472.

Knappke, Othmar, C.PP.S. *Theory of Species Sensibiles.* Ph.D. Dissertation. The Catholic University of America. Washington: The Catholic University of America Press, 1915.

La Drière, J. Craig. "Voice and Address." *Dictionary of World Literature.* Edited by Joseph T. Shipley. New York: The Philosophical Library, 1943.

Maher, Michael, S.J. *Psychology: Empirical and Rational.* New York: Longmans, Green and Company, 1923.

Marsh, George. *Origin and History of the English Language.* New York: Charles Scribner, 1862.

Mätzner, Eduard. *Altenglische Sprachproben.* Berlin: Weidmann'sche Buchhandlung, 1867. Volume I.

Mills, Laurens. *One Soul in Bodies Twain.* Bloomington: Principia Press, 1937.

Moore, Dom Thomas V., O.S.B. *Dynamic Psychology.* Philadelphia: J. B. Lippincott Company, 1924.

Ostler, H. *Die Psychologie des Hugo von St. Viktor, BGPM,* VI, 1. Münster: Aschendorf, 1912.

Patterson, Frank (ed.). *Works of John Milton.* New York: Columbia University Press, 1931. Volume I, Part I.

Pearson, Lu Emily. *Elizabethan Love Conventions.* Berkeley: University of California Press, 1933.

Pegis, A. "In Defense of St. Augustine," *The New Scholasticism,* XVIII (1944), 97-122.

Prescott, Frederick C. *The Poetic Mind.* New York: The Macmillan Company, 1922.

Rank, Otto. *Art and Artist: Creative Urge and Personality Development.* New York: Tudor Publishing Company, 1932.

Savage, Henry. "Hunting in the Middle Ages," *Speculum,* VIII (1933), 30-41.

Schofield, W. H. *English Literature from the Norman Conquest to Chaucer.* New York: The Macmillan Company, 1906.

Sharp, D. E. *Franciscan Philosophy at Oxford in the Thirteenth Century.* Oxford: University Press, 1930.

Small, John (ed.). *The Poems of William Dunbar.* Edinburgh: Blackwood, 1893. Volume II.

Spencer, Theodore. "Chaucer's Hell: A Study in Medieval Conventions," *Speculum,* II (1927), 177-200.

Stanford, Mabel. "Sumnour's Tale," *JEGP,* XIX (1920), 377-381.

Sypherd, Wilbur O. *Studies in Chaucer's House of Fame.* London: Camden Society, 1907.

Taylor, A. "A Metaphor of the Human Body in Literature and Tradition." *Corona. Studies in Celebration of the 80th Birthday of Samuel Singer.* Durham: Duke University Press, 1941, pp. 1-3.

Turner, G. J. (ed.). *Select Pleas of the Forest.* London: Selden Society, 1901. Volume XIII.

Van Os, Arnold. *Religious Visions: The Development of the Eschatological Elements in Medieval Religious Literature.* Amsterdam: H. J. Paris, 1932.

Varnhagen, Hermann (ed.). *Un Samedi par Nuit. Erlanger Beiträge zur Englischen Philologie* (1889), Part I. Appendix I, 114-196.

Wells, J. E. *A Manual of Writings in Middle English,* 1050-1400. New Haven: Yale University Press, 1916.

Willard, Rudolph. "The Address of the Soul to the Body." *PMLA,* L (1935), 957-983.

Wright, Thomas. *St. Patrick's Purgatory: An Essay on the Legends of Purgatory, Hell, and Paradise.* London: John Russell Smith, 1844.

―――. *Latin Poems Commonly attributed to Walter Mapes.* London: Camden Society, 1841.

Greek and Latin Texts

St. Albert the Great. *Opera Omnia.* Edited by A. Borgnet. Paris: Vives, 1890-1899. Volume V.

Aristotle. *De Anima.* Edited with an English Translation by W. S. Hett. Loeb Library. Cambridge: Harvard University Press, 1935.

St. Augustine. *Opera Omnia. PL.* Volumes 32-47.

Bardenhewer, M. O. *Hermetis Trismegisti de castigatione animæ libellum.* Inaugural Dissertation. Bonnæ, 1873.

Baur, Ludwig (ed.). *Die Philosophischen Werke des Robert Grosseteste, BGPM,* IX. Münster: Aschendorf, 1912.

Bede. *Ecclesiastica Historia.* With English Translation by J. E. King. Loeb Library. London: G. Putnam's Sons, 1930. Volume II.

Boethius. *Consolations of Philosophy.* Edited with an English Translation by H. F. Stewart and E. K. Rand. Loeb Library. Cambridge: Harvard University Press, 1936.

Cassian. *De Cœnobiorum Institutis Libri Duodecim,* Bks. IV to XII; *PL,* XLIX.

Gregory the Great. *Moralia,* XXXI; *PL,* LXXVI, 621.

―――. *Dialogues* IV; *PL,* LXXVII, 400.

Hugh of St. Victor. *Summa Sententiarum,* I. *PL,* CLXXVI.

―――. *De Sacramentis Christianæ Fidei, PL,* CLXXV.

John de Bromyard. *Summa Predicantium.* Basle: John of Amorbach, 1487. Volume I.

Philo (Judæus). *Works*. Edited with an English Translation by F. H. Colson and G. H. Whitaker. Loeb Library. New York: G. Putnam's Sons, 1929. Volumes I and II.

Plato. *Alcibiades*. Edited with English Translation by W. R. M. Lamb. Loeb Library. New York: G. Putnam's Sons, 1929. Volume VIII.

———. *Laws*. Edited with English Translation by R. Bury. Loeb Library. New York: G. Putnam's Sons, 1926. Volume II.

———. *Phædo*. Edited with English Translation by H. Fowler. Loeb Library. New York: G. Putnam's Sons, 1929. Volume I.

———. *Phædrus*. Edited with English Translation by H. Fowler. Loeb Library. New York: G. Putnam's Sons, 1929. Volume I.

———. *Timæus*. Edited with English Translation by R. Bury. Loeb Library. New York: G. Putnam's Sons, 1929. Volume VII.

Plotinus. *The Ethical Treatises Being the Treatise of the First Ennead*. Translated into English by Stephen MacKenna. Boston: The Medici Society, Limited, 1917. Volume I.

———. *On the Nature of the Soul Being the Fourth Ennead*. Translated into English by Stephen MacKenna. Boston: The Medici Society, Limited, 1924. Volume IV.

Plutarch. *Moralia*. Edited by G. N. Bernardakis. Leipzig: B. G. Teubner, 1896. Volume VII.

St. Bonaventure. *Opera Omnia*. Edited by St. Bonaventure College. Quaracchi: The College Press, 1882-1902. Volume I.

St. John Chrysostom. *Homilies on the Epistles of St. Paul to the Romans*. V, XIII; PG, XXVIII.

St. Thomas Aquinas. *Opera Omnia*. Edited by E. Frette and P. Mare. Paris: Vives, 1872-1880. Volumes I-XIV.

Wrobel, J. (ed.). *Platonis Timæus interprete Chalcidio cum ejusdem commentario*. Leipzig: B. G. Teubner, 1876.

INDEX

Adams, Joseph Q., 36n.
Aelfric, 29
Alanus de Insulis, 39n.
Albert the Great, St., 34n., 45
Alcuin, 47n., 83
Allen, Beatrice, 1n.
Allison, Tempe E., "On the Body and Soul Legend in the *Castle of Perseverance*," vn.
Ancient Laws and Institutes of England, 13n.
Ancren Riwle, 48n.
Anglo-Saxon Dictionary, 65
Apocalypse of St. Paul, 20
Apocalypse of St. Peter, 21
Aristotle, *De Anima*, 34, 40
Augustine, St., *Confessions*, 48; *De Civitate Dei*, 35; *De Genesi ad Litteram*, 49n., 55; *De Moribus Ecclesiæ*, 1, 36; *De Musica*, 49n.; *De Ordine*, 11, 36; *De Quantitate Animæ*, 42; *De Trinitate*, 46, 47n.; *Epistle*, clxvi, 43n.; *Retractiones*, 28n.; *Soliloquies*, 43

Bardenhewer, M. O., *Hermetis Trismegisti de castigatione animæ libellum*, 32-34 passim; see Hermes Trismegistus
Baruch, 13n.
Batiouchkof, Thomas, 13n., 25, 34n.
Baumgartner, 39n.
Baur, L., 38n., 39n.-40n.
Becker, E., 19n., 24n., 30n.
Bede, 30n.
Berners, Dame Juliana, *The Boke of St. Albans*, 16
Blickling Homilies of the Tenth Century, 13n., 15n.
Blickling Homilies, 77
Boethius, *Consolations of Philosophy*, 51
Bonaventure, St., 46n.
Book of Job, 77

Bourke, Vernon, 49n.
Brennan, Robert, O.P., 56
Brennan, Sister Rose Emmanuella, 40
Bromyard, John de; see John de Bromyard
Brown, Carleton, 1
Buchholz, Richard, 15n.
Burlesque tournament and hunt, 4-5, 19-27

Cædmon, "Song of Creation," 5
Capellanus, Andreas, *Art of Courtly Love*, 17, 18n.
Cassian, *De Institutis*, 65n.
Castle of Perseverance, v.
Chalcidius, 45-46
Child, F. J., *Debate of the Body and the Soul*, 1n.
Cicero, *Somnium Scipionis*, 5; *De Republica*, 5
Collins, Sister M. Emmanuel, O.S.F., vi, 3n., 4
"Comus"; see *Works of John Milton*
Confession theme in *The Debate*, 70-73 passim, 78
Concupiscence: struggle against threefold foes; see Devil, flesh, world
Coogan, Sister Mary Philippa, B.V.M., vn., 36
Cooke, Bernard J., S.J., 42n.-43n.
Courtly love, 17-19
Cyril of Alexandria, 13n.

Dante, A., *Inferno*, 11n.
Debate between the Body and the Soul: date of, 3; history of, 1-2; nature of, 3-5; structure of, 7-31
Demers, G. Ed., 51n.
De Spiritu et Anima, 39n., 55n., 83
Devil, 20-21, 63, 65-66, 69, 71-74, 85

111

De Wulf, Maurice, 31n., 38n.-39n.
Dictionary of World Literature, "Debat," 3n., 4; "Voice and Address," 7n.
Didron, Adolphe N., Christian Iconography, 25
Dream-motif, 5-7
Dudley, Louise, 20n., 24n., 25
Dunbar, William, 19n.

Early English Homilies, 73n.
Early Latin Debate, MS Royal 7 A III, 13n.; see Henningham, Eleanor K.
Eleanor of Aquitaine, 18
English Lyrics of the Thirteenth Century, 8, 23
Ephræm the Syrian, 13n.
Erthe Upon Erthe, 15n.

Flesh, 63, 65-72 passim, 85
Form: first corporeal, 38-40, 52; substantial, 40-47 passim
Friendship, 18-19

Gasquet, Abbot, 65n.
General judgment, 22, 80-81
Gilson, Etienne, 13n., 45n.
Gregory the Great, 17, 47n.; Dialogues, 28n.; Moralia, 65
Grosseteste, Robert, "Castle of Love," 71; "De Intelligentiis," 40n.; "De Luce," 38-39; "De Statu Causarum," 40; Hexæmeron, 39

Hanford, James, H., "Debate of the Heart and Eye," 3n.
Hawking, 14, 16
Heesch, J., 3n.
Hell: location of, 28-29; punishment of, 29-30
Henningham, Eleanor K., vi; "Old English Predecessors of the Worcester Fragments," 8n., 13n.; Early Latin Debate, MS Royal 7 A III, 13n.
Hermes Trismegistus, De Castigatione Animæ, 31-32, 34

Hoccleve, Thomas, Minor Poems of the Vernon Manuscript, 71n.; Regement of Princes and Fourteen Minor Poems, 59n.
Holmes, Urban T., 18
Homilies of the Anglo-Saxon Church, 29
Horse-and-rider analogy: in relation to the essence of man, 12, 24, 35-36, 41-46 passim, 56-57, 83; in relation to the ordering of man, 12, 24, 31-33, 36-37, 57-59, 61, 76, 81-82, 84-85
Hugh of St. Victor, De Sacramentis, 42-43; Summa Sententiarum, 46n., 51, 55
Huizinga, J., 10n.
Hunting as a sport, 14-16; beasts of the chase, 16-17; beasts of venery, 16-17; music of hunt, 26-28

Intelligence in The Debate, 50-51
Isaiah, 13n.
Isidore of Seville, 47n., 83

Jacob's Well, 7n., 22n.
John de Bromyard, Summa Predicantium, 24n.
John Chrysostom, St., 32, 83
Judgment; see general and particular judgment

Keeler, Leo W., 39n.
Ker, W. P., 17n.
Kirby, Thomas A., 18n.
Kittredge, G. L., 1
Knappke, Othmar, 49n.
Kunze, Otto, Þe Desputisoun bitwen þe Bodi and þe Soule, 3

La Drière, J. C., 7n.; see Dictionary of World Literature
Laymon, Brut or Chronicle of Britain, 64n.
Linow, Wilhelm, Þe Desputisoun bitwen þe Bodi and þe Soule, 1n., 2-3
Liturgical act and prayers, 70
Love, courtly; see Courtly love
Luke xvi: 39, 70

Macrobius, 5
Maher, Michael, S.J., 7n.
Mankind, 36
Marie of Champagne, 18
Marsh, George, 3n.
Master of Game, 26n.-27n.
Matthew xv: 14, 70
Mätzner, Eduard, 2, 3n.
Middle English Sermons, 66, 71n., 73
Middle English Reader, 2, 5n., 87n.
Mills, Laurens, 19
Moore, Dom Thomas V., O.S.B., 7n.
Moses, 32
Motor-and-boat image: in relation to unity of man, 12; in relation to the ordering of man, 12
Myrc, John, *Festial*, 67n.

New English Dictionary, 48, 52n., 59n., 77n.
Noctis sub Silencio Tempore Brumali, 20n., 50n., 71

"Old English Address of the Lost Soul to Body," 15, 71
Old English Homilies, 16n., 26n., 71, 73, 74n.
Old English Miscellany, 30n.
Ostler, H., 47n.
Ovid, 17-18

Particular judgment, 80-81
Paul, St., *Epistles*, 13n., 32, 61, 67
Pearson, Lu Emily, 18
Pegis, A., 42n.
Penance as satisfaction for sin, 70, 72-73, 78
Philip the Chancellor, 39n.
Philo (Judæus), *Works*, 32-33, 83
Plato, *Alcibiades*, 42; *De Anima*, 34; *Dialogues*, 32; *Laws*, 48; *Phædo*, 9-10, 19n., 32; *Phædrus*, 32, 47; *Timæus*, 43, 45n., 54
Plotinus, *Enneads*, 34-35, 44n.

Plutarch, *Moralia*, 35, 83
Powers of the soul, 46-54 *passim*
Prescott, Frederick, *The Poetic Mind*, 6, 7n.
Pricke of Conscience, 28n.
Pride of Life, v.

Ramsay, Robert Lee, vn.
Rank, Otto, *Art and Artist*, 6
Reason in *The Debate*, 50-51
Redemption, 77
Rhaban, Maur, 47n., 83
Rider-and-horse analogy; see horse-and-rider analogy
Rolle, Richard, "A tretyse of gostly batayle," 37; see *Yorkshire Writers: Richard Rolle and His Followers*

Savage, Henry, 16, 17n.
Schofield, W. H., 1
Senses, classification of, 48-49; mortification of, 67
Seven deadly sins; see sin
Sharp, D. E., 39n.
Ship-and-helmsman image, 33-34, 56; *see also* motor-and-boat and horse-and-rider images
Sin: original sin and consequences, 60-62; seven deadly sins, 64-66; sources of: threefold concupiscence, 65-75 *passim*
Skelton, John, *Magnyfycence*, vn.
Soul of man: animating and first principle, 40; form of body, 40-41; manner of presence in body, 45-46; origin, 54; unity; see union of soul and body
Speculum Sacerdotale, 37
Spencer, Theodore, 29-30
Stanford, Mabel, 79n.
St. Patrick's Purgatory, 29n.-30n.
Story of Genesis and Exodus, 64n.
Sypherd, Wilbur O., 5

Taylor, A., "A Metaphor of the Human Body in Literature and Tradition," 45n.
Temptation: sources of; see Devil, flesh, world

Thomas Aquinas, St., *Quæstiones Disputatæ: De Malo*, 5, 6n.; *De Anima*, 56n.; *Sentences*, 45-46; *Summa Contra Gentiles*, 41, 44, 46-47, 49, 52; *Summa Theologica*, 22, 41, 49, 52, 54-56, 61, 65, 68-69, 72n.-73n., 74-75, 78n., 81n., 84; *Trinity and Unicity of the Intellect*, 40
Three foes of man; see Devil, flesh, world
Tournament, burlesque; see Burlesque tournament and hunt
Twelfth Century Homilies, 13n., 66n., 73

Ubi Sunt? motif, 12-14, 31, 65, 75
Union of soul and body: accidental union, 12, 44-47 *passim*; essential union, 44-47 *passim*
Un Samedi par Nuit, 13n., 25, 34n., 50n., 71

Van Os, Arnold, 21n., 26
Varro, 35, 83
Vercelli Homilien, 13n., 16n.
Villon, François, 13
Visio Fulberti; see *Noctis sub Silencio Tempore Brumali*

Vision of Thurcill, 19
Vision of Tundale, 20, 25-26
Voice and Address; see *Dictionary of World Literature*

Wells, J. E., 1n.
Willard, Rudolph, 13n.
William of Auvergne, 47n., 83
Will in *The Debate*, 53-54
William of St. Thierry, 47n., 83
Wit in *The Debate;* see intelligence
Works of John Milton, The, 9
Worcester Fragments, 15, 50n., 71
World, 63, 65-66, 69, 71-72, 74-75, 85
Wright, Thomas, *Latin Poems Commonly attributed to Walter Mapes*, 2, 3n., 20n., 70n.; *St. Patrick's Purgatory: An Essay on the Legends of Purgatory, Hell, and Paradise*, 11, 19n., 21n.
Wrobel, J., *Platonis Timæus interprete Chalcidio cum ejusdem commentario;* see Chalcidius
Yorkshire Writers: Richard Rolle and His Followers, 30n., 37

CPSIA information can be obtained at www.ICGtesting.com
Printed in the USA
LVOW07s1454030913

350793LV00009B/136/P